extraordinary

STORIES OF ADOPTING
CHILDREN WITH DOWN SYNDROME

Compiled by:
CADY DRIVER

Foreword by:
MEREDITH TOERING

JPV PRESS
STORY. PRESERVED.

Cover photography © Jackie Beachy Photography, 2019.

Open Hearts for Orphans photo © Just to See You Smile.

Printed in the United States of America

First Printing, 2019

ISBN 978-1-946389-14-5

JPV PRESS

STORY. PRESERVED.

2106 Main Street / PO Box 201, Winesburg, OH 44690

www.jpvpress.com

FOR THE KIDS

TaBLe OF ConTenTS

i   *We Believe...*

iii   *Foreword*

VX   *Preface*

1   Open Hearts for Orphans

13   Lian's Story

31   Edie's Story

49   Penelope's Story

65   Elliott's Story

79   The Blended Bunch

97   His Name is Samuel

115   Kai's Story

133   Sam's Story: When The Road Darkens

147   Adeline's Story

165   Worth's Story

181   Lucy, Henry, and Eloise's Story

199   MinLan and John Preston's Story

215   National Down Syndrome Adoption Network

221   *Resource Guide*

245   *Acknowledgments*

we Believe...

we Believe every child deserves the love and nurturing of a family.

we Believe in embracing, enjoying, and sharing this one special life and all the blessings we have been given.

we Believe in celebrating each child's milestones and every small step in between.

we Believe in helping children dream big, reach toward possibilities, and be courageous.

we Believe sharing knowledge, insight, and experiences with others can build a community of acceptance, support, and encouragement.

we Believe this world and all the places in it are big enough for everyone, even when one person's needs and abilities look different than another's.

we Believe families that adopt a child with Down syndrome are not saints nor have superpowers. They are only ordinary families choosing to make a difference.

we Believe children who have that something "extra" and the "ordinary" families who adopt them create a beautiful picture of something *Extraordinary.*

Foreword

It was the coldest January night when she came to me on a train—I'll never forget the chill. She was bundled in blankets, but even through their weight, I could feel the wisp of her. The baby girl placed in my arms that January night was eleven months old and weighed less than eight pounds. As I unwrapped the blankets to meet my newest brave heart, her eyes caught mine, and her gaunt little face stretched into the sweetest grin, eyes crinkling into half-moons.

I named her Lilah Lu, and the girl's broken heart soon owned the hearts of us all... we were smitten by her courage, her fight, and her tiny iron will. You see, I live in China and run a medical foster home for orphans with literal broken hearts. As they come from one corner of the country to the other, we receive these brave and broken-hearted babes in Beijing with open arms and waiting hearts, knowing that ours will never again be the same.

In this little House of Brave, as we've come to be known, warriors sleep in cribs and go to battle for every beat. Each heart beats brave and with its own sort of tune, and we run right alongside them—chasing that song of hope.

Lilah thrived in our home as we sat day-by-day, hour-by-hour, by her side. We fed her by syringe, milliliter by tiny milliliter, until her body could finally tolerate a full bottle. She slowly became stronger, growing both in weight and in trust, that sneaking smile I saw the first day now a permanent fixture on her little pixie face. In addition to our Lilah's broken little heart, she was born with very sick lungs and an extra copy of her twenty-first chromosome... Down syndrome. We knew our little Lu girl was in for the fight of her life, and she showed up to the battle with a fierceness that defied all odds and expectations. I am so proud of my girl. She was so very brave.

Sometimes stories read the way you had hoped, and sometimes they really just don't. Although our Lilah gave absolutely everything she had, she peacefully passed away, her life and her death a miracle that sparked ripples around the world. You see, Lilah's courage dared a whole lot of people to be brave—to step out of their comfort zones, to ask the hard questions they had never before entertained, to let themselves fall head-over-heart in love with an eight-pound baby girl who never would have been part of their plan. Her courage became a challenge to those families who were ready to throw their fears, their caution, and their plans to the wind—to say, "We choose you, Little One. We choose you."

In the short time this little Braveheart was part of my home, over one hundred families stepped forward to inquire about her adoption. Over one hundred mamas and daddies hoped to bring her home. One hundred families gave their hearts to the babe across the world and said, "You are seen, you are known, you are worthy, and we want to call you ours, and we will be yours, forever and always." Lilah's story did not write itself the way I had hoped at all. I walked out of that hospital with empty arms and broken dreams for the future of this warrior girl for whom I had hoped all things, but I could never have dreamed the impact her story would have.

Stories have the power to shape us, to change us, to open our hearts and make us new. Lilah's story did just that. Today, because of Lilah, there are thirty-eight new sons and daughters around this world, thirty-eight families formed, thirty-eight children—with Down syndrome and that brave warrior heart—adopted. Because of her story, her fight, her hope, and her LIFE, others just like her are now home. Chosen. Loved. Cherished. Named.

Her story changed the world, and the stories you will find in these pages have the power to do the same. We all have a story, and we get to choose how it's lived. Brene Brown believes that we have two choices in this life—we can either choose comfort, or we can choose courage. The stories that follow are full to the brim of unbridled courage, of all the hope and hard and joy and faith that happen when you let go of the life you thought you wanted, and run hard into the one you never expected. I think you'll find it's the kind of life for which you've always been waiting.

Hope never comes with guarantees, but it is more important than every fear, worth more than every risk. In death and in life, in love and in loss, in grief and in joy, hope always remains. When you let go of the known to free-fall into the unknown, it can be terrifying beyond words, but oh, friends, it is good. These following words will move you and mark you, and I promise that you will put this book down, forever changed. May we let these stories dare us to be brave, to choose courage, and to seek the joy in the unexpected. May we—with arms held high and eyes wide open—jump straight into the life we were always meant to live.

Whatever that life may be, whatever that choice may be… I dare you, friends; I dare you to be brave.

- Meredith Toering
Morning Star Foundation

preface

It is an honor to share with you the stories of these families and their journey to saying "Yes" to their precious children. Since starting our publishing company, it became our number one goal to release a book containing stories of families who have adopted a child or children with Down syndrome.

We didn't begin our journey to specifically adopt children with special needs, but as we completed our home study paperwork, our prayers began to change. We went from asking the Lord to please give us children to asking Him to bring us the children who needed us the most, and praying He would equip us to meet their needs.

We now have four children, all of whom are adopted and have special needs. Our oldest son has Autism Spectrum Disorder, and our youngest three children all have Down syndrome.

Just a few weeks after our home study was approved, we were matched with our oldest son. He was almost four years old, and a diagnosis had not yet been completed. The first year was challenging but also held many times of joy.

A few years later, our agency called to ask if we would consider adopting a baby girl, yet to be born, with Down syndrome. We were excited to say, "Yes!" In less than two weeks, she was in our arms. Her beginning was a bumpy one, with an extended NICU stay, several surgeries, some complications, and a feeding tube. We were thrilled to finally bring her home and settle in as a family of four.

Welcoming our daughter into our family also opened our eyes to just how big the need is for families willing to open their hearts and their homes to children with Down syndrome. (There are hundreds of children with Down syndrome worldwide waiting for a forever family.) We joined the NDSAN (National Down Syndrome Adoption Network) registry after our daughter turned two years old.

Six months later, we were matched with our son. He was born several states away, and after a brief stay in the NICU, he was discharged from the hospital. We spent the next week enjoying our vacation home-away-from-home while we waited for the ICPC to be completed.

Although we thought our family was complete, we welcomed another baby boy (our third child with Down syndrome) in a very unexpected open adoption placement. We finalized his adoption when he was eight months old, and absolutely adore him. We are so thankful for each of the children God has brought us. They are tremendous blessings, and we cannot imagine our lives without them.

The royalties from this book will be given to Open Hearts for Orphans. This will help fund their "Say Yes" adoption grants for families adopting a child with Down syndrome.

- Marlin and Lisa

CHAPTER
ONE

OPEN HEARTS FOR ORPHANS

Our personal story does not include Down syndrome, but it does have adoption written all over it. My husband and I have five extra-precious blessings, all adopted internationally from China. Our family-building journey began back in 2005 when there was an identified need to bring home healthy infant girls. My husband had remembered, as a teenager, learning about the "Dying Rooms" in China, where countless little lives were lost merely because of their gender.

The minute adoption became a subject in our home, Jim made it clear that it was definitely an option he wanted to explore. Though the seed hadn't been planted in my heart the same way, I knew—somehow—that my motherhood wouldn't come from my own womb, and that never bothered me. I was 100 percent on board with God's plan, since pregnancy obviously wasn't part of it, so we entered a new territory called the adoption process.

We were matched with our first little treasure named "Xiaoyuan" (pronounced "Sh-ow U-en") meaning "intelligence, brightness, and beauty" in 2006. That's when we first discovered how we could so naturally, and easily, fall in love with a child long before we'd even met them—with that little seed called "Yes" that sprouts into a winding adoption process and then wildly blossoms when you lay eyes and hands upon that little human being for the first time. There's always a unique and complex mix of emotions involved, ranging from an unexplainable level of fear to an inconceivable new level of joy. We stared at her picture for days on end and named our daughter-to-be Madolyn Olivia.

After a three-month wait that seemed like years, she was perfect in every way when we finally held her in our aching arms—a robust and beautiful brown-skinned baby who'd been blessed with the love of a foster family in China. She gobbled down Cheerios and grieved in her own quiet way as we navigated our new roles in her world. Baby Madi fit like a glove into our lives, and she's lived up to her Chinese name in every sense. That child tapped into an overflowing source of love in our hearts that we hadn't even realized was within us. She opened the floodgates to new life in our souls.

In 2008, we felt it was the right time for a sibling after settling into our new-parent status for a couple of years, and we started the adoption process again. By that time, some rules and shifts had taken place in China, and healthy infant girls were—thankfully—being adopted domestically. That new trend in China's culture, however, began to leave a growing number of abandoned boys. Many of them had moderate to severe special needs that their birthparents likely couldn't afford to treat.

When our agency approached us with the gender option, we were perfectly willing to bring home a boy, and in January of 2010, we traveled back to China to adopt our first son, Daniel. He was two years old at the time and living with congenital heart disease; specifically, Tetralogy of Fallot (a combination of four heart defects). He was the most beautiful child—milky white skin, cherry red lips (when they weren't blue from his heart disease), and enormous, soulful, dark brown eyes.

Despite the unknowns involved, our hearts were both beating to the drum of hope, and my husband and I knew that our "Yes" was the only answer to that most honorable call to parent another child. We brought Daniel home and enjoyed a quiet life of cocooning, bonding, and creating memories for four months. He had the sweetest voice that sounded soft and scratchy, somewhat like Elmo, and it was nearly impossible not to give in to his every whim.

Although I, in my over-protective ways, constantly attempted to keep Daniel in a bubble, I also knew I was squelching his ability to live life like a typical toddler. My husband, on the other hand, treated Daniel with all the ruggedness that a big and burly Papa Bear would, and our son adored the chance to be a little thrill-seeker. At times, we both longed to pack him up and drive far, far away to avoid his operation, but we knew his anatomy desperately needed correction to give him a chance at long life.

Our son's open-heart surgery took place on May 11, 2010, and though our boy came out of surgery strong, he went into cardiac arrest the next morning, and we spent the following nineteen days fighting for Daniel's life. There were days that we saw miracles in his improvement, and there were days of organ failures and setbacks that brought us to our knees.

Daniel never came home from that hospital. His tired body just couldn't take it anymore, and he left us for Heaven on Trinity Sunday. It was the most dark and raging storm of our lives, leaving a path of sheer devastation, including a four-year-old sister who could barely process the grim reality of not having her little brother to spoil. We never lost hope, though, and the Lord showed up for us constantly with signs of His goodness and faithfulness. Daniel was a blessing beyond measure, and he'd transformed our souls just by being in our lives. We were thankful that he did not die alone; he was a beloved son, brother, grandson, godson, and nephew. How blessed I am to be called his earthly mother.

Amidst the most intense pain we'd ever experienced, the Holy Spirit seared two things into my heart. The first was, "Share his story," so I penned Daniel's short life in our family into a memoir called, *With an Open Heart*, and preserved every scrap of detail I could remember about Daniel, and how he changed us. The royalties from my labor of love were designated to be donated, in Daniel's memory, to orphan-care ministries. The second message was, "Go back," and we were scared—beyond scared—to say "Yes" again, but we knew that familiar tug of the Holy Spirit in our hearts, and our obedience led us straight to another son.

Less than a year later, we were China-bound on an airplane to bring home our son Charlie, an eighteen-month-old baby with a reported heart defect. Bringing another child home didn't replace Daniel, and we never expected that to happen. It did, however, manage to bring fresh, new joy to our hearts. We knew that Daniel would've wanted that for our family. We also knew he would've wished that future upon another child, since we had room in our home and in our hearts. By the time we arrived in China for Charlie, his heart defect had spontaneously healed, and he was a healthy little baby who simply needed nurturing and nourishment in order to thrive.

Life was grand with just our two little ones until one Sunday morning in December 2012, when we sat in a pew and listened to a homily about the Holy Family. That message we heard about the sacred significance of the parent/child relationship between Joseph, Mary, and Jesus shot straight into my heart, and I knew the Lord was calling us to open our hearts again. My husband immediately shot the idea down, thinking I'd lost my mind, since we had about zero funds to spare, but I begged him to trust in God's financial provision for a child. I promised that I would handle every detail of the fundraising.

Jim begrudgingly agreed to start another process, but I knew those hard feelings would soften on his giant teddy bear interior. The Lord did provide financially through the hands and hearts of many loving friends, and although we had envisioned another daughter in our family, we were matched with a five-and-a-half-year-old little boy named Xiao Xiao on March 18, 2014. It was new territory, with a medical diagnosis of clubbed feet, which we would discover was much less scary than it sounded.

We were entering the new world of older child adoption, which brought an entirely different set of learning curves than adopting a baby. Xiao Xiao's photo revealed an unmistakable sadness in his eyes that screamed, "Love me," and so we would. We gave him his new name, Joseph, the day after we received his file, which happened to be the Feast day of St. Joseph, a day in our faith honoring the ultimate foster father to the son of God.

Joseph became an official member of our family in China on his brother Charlie's birthday, September 16, and he was baptized in December 2014 at the Feast of the Holy Family—the same service where the seed of adoption had been planted in my heart exactly two years earlier. It felt like such a full-circle miracle! Charlie and Joseph have been "twinned" for the most part, and they truly are Oscar and Felix of the Odd Couple (showing my age). God could not have matched them more perfectly as brothers.

In my heart, though, I knew we weren't done. I truly felt the Lord telling me there was *still* room for one more in the nest—maybe it was that one empty seat in our van; perhaps it was the uneven number of kids for our family outings, or maybe it was the extra spot at the dinner table. It was a void that simply needed to be filled. My husband was feeling the "fear" factor again, though, and voiced his reluctance, for fear of financial wreckage. It's a paralyzing word, isn't it? It can lead to a host of detrimental thoughts like, *How can we ever afford this? Is it possible for us to love this child who doesn't share our DNA? Will we ruin our other kids by adopting?* These fears can be real and present factors, and each one of our adoptions has been almost like climbing a faith-ladder to overcome the paralysis.

One by one, we climbed another rung and faced those fears head-on. They were all limitations that *we put on ourselves,* and God's plans were obviously so much better than ours. In typical fashion, with a heart the size of a planet, Jim changed his mind after he'd prayed and prayed about it. He simply couldn't deny that we had "enough" to give to another child.

In 2016, we brought home our littlest love, Lulu. She, like Joseph, was almost six when we were united with her. Though our spitfire daughter has the somewhat scary-sounding diagnosis of cerebral palsy, it is a label that does not define her—this girl is as determined and strong as the day is long. She amazes us constantly with her confidence and perseverance. She has managed to make leaps and bounds of progress in the two years since we brought her home.

After Lulu's adoption, Jim and I both knew we were "on hold" to bring home any more children, for lack of resources and our older age. I'll never utter the words "We're done"; however, our nest finally felt complete, and I heard the Lord say, "You've worked ten years to build your family, now go live and enjoy each other." But as someone whose eyes have been opened, I couldn't dare stop there. On May 30, 2016, six years after our Daniel had left us to be with Jesus, Open Hearts for Orphans was born—the beauty from ashes non-profit organization created in our son Daniel's memory.

It is an incredible gift to do this work, and it is an honor to serve the most vulnerable of God's children. I'll never understand why the Lord never made a way—in five adoption trips to China—for my husband and me to visit an orphanage. We were denied a visit from three of our children's orphanages, and two of the institutions were at least four hours away, so we made a decision—based on a gut feeling after meeting our children—that the road trip would have been difficult on both of them.

I dream that, someday, we will make a return trip to the birth country of our children and see inside the walls of an orphanage, but this is the time to serve the children who still remain hopelessly without families. I imagine we'll be changed in more ways than I could possibly fathom from that experience when it finally happens.

Our charity's mission has always been divided into three areas of need: medical intervention for orphaned children, meeting the basic needs of orphaned children, and providing financial assistance for adoptive families through our "Say Yes" adoption grant program. Among other accomplishments, we have been able to help fund heart surgeries, provide life-saving medical equipment to medical foster homes, assist with care and expenses for two orphanages (one in China and one in Tanzania), and we issued seven of our "Say Yes" grants in 2017. We are on track to exceed that in 2018, and we pray the Lord multiplies our charitable successes!

You might be wondering where our story and Open Hearts for Orphans fits into this special project dedicated to families who've been blessed by children with Down syndrome. I feel like I've always been drawn to people with special needs, Down syndrome included, as I reflect on various encounters of my life. It's never made sense to me that people could be unkind to people with special needs when they were created in the image of God, just like you and me.

Through the years, I've followed the stories and have become friends, through social media, with numerous families who have adopted children with Down syndrome. I've always known that children with Down syndrome are special gifts from the Lord. Those two letters stand for "Delightfully Special" in my mind, and I believe that extra chromosome is a little gift from God—an extra measure of sweetness to their human recipe. I love how they seem to see the world through a more heavenly lens—they have the ability to filter out hatred and meanness more easily than the average person can. That trait is a gift from above, I believe, to remind us how we should act on this road called life. I know it's not all rainbows and unicorns in families with special needs (any family, really) but they seem to possess a special innocence, and I just adore that about them.

In the summer of 2017, I felt more drawn to orphaned children with Down syndrome than ever. One reason, I recall, was an article that was shared about how Down syndrome has almost disappeared in Iceland because of ultrasound use and abortion. The fact that an entire country on our globe would choose to negate and destroy the lives of these precious gifts from God just wrecked me, and I became determined to make orphans with Down syndrome a specific part of our Open Hearts for Orphans fundraising mission in 2018 and beyond. Lo and behold, the Lord made a clear path in early 2018 and brought a lovely adoptive mama into my life named Cady Driver. I was immediately drawn to her creative mind and artistic hand through Facebook, and when I discovered that she'd adopted the most adorable little boy with Down syndrome, I imagined and hoped for a partnership to serve orphans with Down syndrome together.

Cady and I collaborated well and created a special shirt campaign that we called "Downright Lovable." She inked the perfect design, and we raised enough funds to give three of our "Say Yes" grants to families adopting children with Down syndrome. We are more than grateful that the royalties for this labor of love you hold in your hands will be donated to our non-profit organization, and we are committed to designating those funds for orphans with Down syndrome and the families who run to adopt them.

We hope you find abundant inspiration through these shared stories of the wonderful families who grace the pages of this book, and we appreciate your purchase, which will undoubtedly bless more families and orphaned children with Down syndrome in the future.

- Lisa Murphy

CHAPTER
TWO

Lian's Story

"I think I'm ready to adopt." My husband nodded confidently as he spoke. My heart skipped a beat, then another for good measure, and I didn't move or breathe for fear of frightening that statement away. A thousand prayers and countless tears had led up to this moment, this sweet, simple sentence. Dozens of sleepless nights, wishing, star gazing, willing, begging, pleading with God for this day to come. I longed to hear those words, to see the confidence in his eyes, to feel our momentum change in one accord, one God-spoken direction, one Spirit-willed journey.

This decision was years in the making.

"Take a week to pray about it," I countered. I wanted him to be sure, whole-heartedly sure. I didn't think my heart could take another breath of vacillation. He nodded.

We took a week to pray about it separately, although I must admit that my prayers weren't about whether we should adopt or not. I already knew the answer was to adopt; it had always been to adopt. No, my prayers centered around pure joy and thankfulness, laced with unadulterated excitement.

I was going to be a mother again! Chris and I, Cady, had three biological teenagers, and I couldn't wait! I had it all perfectly planned out in my head. It would be a little girl; she'd be adorable, with straight, black, exclamation-point pigtails. I felt it in my gut that we'd adopt from China. She'd be little, maybe around the age of one. She'd have some minor, manageable special need. *There. It's all laid out for you, God. Make it happen!* And God laughed.

By November, we had settled on an agency, and by December, we were starting the home study process. Now, as a single income, homeschooling family, we really were clueless as to how we were going to pay for this adoption. It was a huge step of faith, especially for Chris, to start this journey without any money set aside, but money means nothing in God's world. Time and again, as fees would approach, God would miraculously provide… a donation here, a garage sale there, a grant received, a successful art sale, etc. Somehow, some way, we made it. Looking back, I'm not entirely sure how it just fell into place. All the glory goes to God for this!

It was towards the end of November, and everyone was in the joyful throes of holiday preparation. One chilly day, our agency contact told us about a "Waiting Child" list that was on the agency's website.

"It's a list of children that we have a harder time finding homes for," she stated. "These children might have more severe special needs."

Hmmm, ok. Should I check this out? I'm not sure. I have this picture in my head, God… I'll just sit down and see.

I started scrolling through the list, and the little faces stared out at me, each one pleading, "Are you my Mama?" Their special needs trailed down the screen; hydrocephalus, Down syndrome, cerebral palsy, cleft palate... The list went on and on.

This is too much, too scary, God; how can I? There are so many children, so many overwhelming needs. Breathing deeply, I was shaking my head. *Why are there so many?* I kept scrolling.

Then, in one life-defining instant, this one little photo popped onto my screen, and my heart stopped. I looked into this child's eyes, and I just knew. He was ours; I was convinced of it! Quickly, I scanned his brief medical paragraph. Alexander, two years old, Down syndrome. My heart dropped.

What would Chris say? Children who have Down syndrome sometimes require a lifetime of care. We had no experience. We had wanted a minor special needs girl and here I was, mooning over a little boy with Down syndrome simply because of a pair of gorgeous eyes and adorable cheeks. I slammed the computer shut. *No. Yes? Should I even ask Chris? Am I crazy?*

I logged in again to look at his sweet photo and re-read his file. I heard Chris's car drive in.

"Hon, there's this little guy on the Waiting Child list, and I know we wanted a girl, but they have a hard time finding homes for boys, and he has Down syndrome, and it could mean a lifetime of care, leukemia, possibly heart problems, therapies, thyroid issues..." I was rambling nervously as I ran out of counting fingers.

My husband stared at the screen. "That's our son!"

I nearly fell off my chair. But... but... yes? We both agreed on this? I couldn't believe it! It couldn't possibly be **this** easy.

We sat down to dinner, but we were both antsy. Was this our

son? Our entire perspective had just shifted.

"Call the agency and get his file," Chris insisted. "Call now!"

Leaving my unfinished dinner, I dialed nervously.

"You're never going to believe this," Tiffany, our agency contact said, "but Alexander's file has sat untouched, un-requested for two whole years. Not one family has been interested in him, but last night, another family pulled his file. He is no longer available unless they say 'No' to him after ten days."

I hung up, heavy-hearted. Alexander had a family who wanted him. He wasn't meant to be ours. Tears pricked my eyes as I shook my head. Chris's eyes dropped.

Over the next few days, I questioned God as to why we had both felt so strongly about Alexander. Why had his little eyes spoken so eloquently to me? Why had Chris been so incredibly sure that Alexander was our son?

Sad and frustrated, I would scold myself. I should be overjoyed that he had a family, finally! Maybe this was just to open our hearts to other special needs that we wouldn't have been open to otherwise. And yet, every day, I would sit in the glow of my screen and look at his beautiful face.

"Stop looking at his photo!" my bestie scolded me. "You're just torturing yourself. God has a different plan for you."

But I kept looking. I couldn't help myself. A mother's heart wants what it wants, and I wanted him.

On December 7, around dinnertime, the phone rang. It was Tiffany.

"SO!" She sounded upbeat. "Remember that little guy that your husband said was your son? Well, the family who was looking at his file returned it. Would you like to pull his file?"

"YES!" I'm pretty sure I shouted. "Yes, please," I stated more meekly.

Suddenly, with Christmas right around the corner, we were in the flurry of locating an international pediatrician and getting the mountain of referral paperwork completed. We learned that Alexander's Chinese name was "Lian Lian." As we were gathering all of our information, I found myself examining that name. Lian Lian.

Once we put this huge packet of paperwork in the mail, we will have officially accepted Lian as ours. Chris was holding the packet as he left for work. "Are you sure? This is it!"

I was sure. He strolled out the door, and it was done. I sat down in front of the Christmas tree in a daze. So much had happened in such a short amount of time. I could hardly believe that we were here at this moment of acceptance.

For so many years, I had felt like Hannah in the Bible, praying, longing, and weeping for another child. It wasn't that I was ungrateful for our three children; I just knew there was another child out there that needed me. I spent many sleepless, tearful nights bargaining with God, begging Him to entrust me with another child. I just knew, deep down inside, that our family wasn't yet complete. I had waited and doubted, prayed and yearned.

Deep in remembrance and thankfulness, I was still in such disbelief. Lian Lian. He will be ours!

I wondered about his name, though… I sat down at the computer and Googled "Chinese name meaning—Lian."

My first search popped up. Lian. What does the name "Lian" mean? The different meanings of the name "Lian" are: God has answered; Lotus; tenderness.

God. Has. Answered.

Goosebumps and chills swept over me. I was overcome, sobbing into my hands. These were tears of joy—mixed with regret—because I had doubted God. I had been unjustly angry, and I had been jealous of other adoptive mothers whose journey seemed so neatly laid out for them. It was as if God was gently saying, "Daughter, why do you doubt me? Don't I always answer? It's not your timing; it's Mine."

Fast forward through a blurry year of paperwork, fundraising, and home studies, and we were finally traveling in October of 2016!

After a few days in Beijing to get over jet lag, our "gotcha day" was set for October 30. It was a Sunday, and we had hardly slept during our trip. In our hotel room, I carefully laid out the few toys I had brought, folding and re-folding the blanket just so in the hotel crib. We were counting down the hours on that Sunday afternoon.

It was time. The orphanage staff brought Lian to the conference room on the top floor of our hotel. The elevator was silent, filled with nervous expectation as we rode up. In my hands were a stuffed giraffe, a snack, and a car. What would he be like? Would he even like us? Could we do this?

God. Has. Answered. Lian Lian.

We stepped off the elevator, hearts pounding, and were led to a set of double doors. On the other side of those doors was our son. I was willing the doors to open. *Maybe if I stare at them long enough, hard enough…*

In a flurry of activity, the doors opened, and the orphanage *ayi* (aunt, nursemaid) carried Lian to us. She was bouncing him, chanting, and pointing at me. "Mama, Mama!" she loudly exclaimed. "Baba, Baba!" pointing at Chris.

I didn't reach for Lian. I had already prepared myself for this moment. He might reject me as the mother. It's very common for the mother to be the rejected parent, and I had readied my heart for this. Lian wouldn't come to me but willingly reached for Chris, somehow making the "I Love You" sign to him with his fingers. I was actually glad of this, his first bond with his father. It was a necessary delay that I was willing to wait on.

I tentatively reached out and stroked his hair. It was like brittle straw, slightly orange-tinted in the window's light. *Malnourishment*, was my first thought. I had yet to hold him, and I was already planning his meals in my head.

We were ushered into the conference room and quickly processed. I was busily signing away, all the while staring at the small, stinky little boy who was sitting on the floor, absorbed in pulling off his shoes. He was so oblivious to the life changes that were happening to him at the moment. So tiny, so alone in the world, adrift at the whim of strangers, governments, and institutions. A voiceless person ferried here and there, another number in the endless stream of inopportune moments and relentless heartbreak.

Papers signed, I scooped him up for the first time. He didn't protest. He felt too small in my arms, too small for his age, too light, too weak. I knew what an almost-three-year-old should feel like. "He's too small."

"At least he's not screaming."

We carried him back to our room, and I discovered that changing a diaper is like riding a bike. You don't really forget how to do it, although the former is a bit more aromatic than the latter.

Now what? Chris and I pondered this small person who was throwing every toy we gave him across the room.

We ordered room service. What did he eat? We had no idea. Noodles seemed a safe choice. There, on the bathroom floor, we attempted to feed him noodles. It was hysterically messy as we fumbled chopsticks, along with an unknown toddler's eating habits. Somehow, noodles found their way into the child as well as onto the carpet, his clothes, our clothes, the bathroom floor, and the towels we were now using as mops. I made a mental note: *We'll leave housekeeping a good tip.*

Bath time was another adventure that we somehow survived by utilizing every last towel available. Lian was quite the baseball pitcher. He threw or rolled absolutely everything. It seemed to be his way of playing, or coping with the unknown.

We finally unpacked his little Mickey Mouse backpack that was handed to us by the staff. In it was a favorite toy that played mandarin songs, a well-worn photo album of our family that we had sent to Lian, some snacks, a new pair of shoes, and an outfit. This was absolutely all he owned. I sat back in tears. It struck me that the photo album was falling apart. His foster mom, to whom we owed a great debt of gratitude, must have looked through the album countless times with him, pointing to each of us. "This is your Mama. This is your Baba. Your brother, your sisters. Here is your house."

I could just picture her with Lian on her lap, selflessly preparing this child that she has loved and cared for to be taken by another family. I'm sure she loved him. How could she not? I know that she took him swimming sometimes; he slept in her bed with her at night, nestled by her side. The few photos we have show him smiling in a clean, neat apartment, playing busily.

On a side note, that toy that plays Mandarin songs? Yes, it plays hundreds of songs, lights up in several colors, and so far, the batteries are still going strong nineteen months after coming home. We suspect that the Chinese are holding out on us in regards to battery quality and duration.

After an uneventful bedtime, with Lian clinging to Chris's arm as he fell asleep, we were able to transfer him to his crib, and thankfully, he slept the night through as we fitfully caught up on our sleep.

As we traveled through all of the week's required appointments, I noticed that Lian absolutely adored Chris, but would merely tolerate me. For some reason, he wouldn't make eye contact with me very much. As glad as I was that Lian and Chris had started off well with bonding, I recognized that I needed to work on as much "attachment" bonding as I could. Hand-feeding Lian while making eye contact, being the one to rock him to sleep, bathe him, and snuggle him will help Lian understand that I am his mother, and will hopefully commence the attachment process.

Several days later, Lian and I finally had our first bonding moment, and it was, appropriately, over a cup of Starbucks coffee. Taking a break from shopping, we had stopped at Starbucks for a delightful coffee/whipped cream treat. I plopped Lian onto a bench, and on a whim, I dipped my finger into the white froth, offering it to him like a mother bird feeding her chick. At that moment our eyes locked, his dark-eyed gaze melting into mine, and I knew we'd be ok. He would eventually come to love me, attach to me, and I already knew that I would give my life for this child. I loved this small stranger with my whole heart, fiercely, despite the spitting, hitting, biting, throwing, and pinching.

Yes, dear reader, if you're wondering if everything was smooth and sparkly; it wasn't. And that's ok. I knew these behaviors were simply orphanage and defensive based, and they would fade away.

And eventually, with lots of time, love, and patience, they did.

When you're in country, you do whatever it takes to make it through. Lollipops, Starbucks whipped cream, stickers everywhere, blowing bubbles during bath time, and good old McDonald's french fries. Oh yes, he loved those!

About four days after we had gotten Lian, he woke up early one morning, sobbing. He hadn't really cried at all since we had gotten him. No crying at bedtime, nap time, no crying when he had to go somewhere or was tired or hungry. He was quiet; busy in his own little world, focused on his shoes, or playing with the strap on the stroller. We had seen a ghost of a grin appear with slow-growing frequency, but no crying. No tears.

As an experienced mom, I knew that crying is something that two-year-olds do often, well, and with vast and varying degrees of enthusiasm.

That 5:45 am cry was different, and as we scrambled out of bed to get him, I had a feeling that this was the beginning of his mourning. Mourning his foster mother with whom he had lived for over a year, mourning the loss of a familiar language, familiar faces, his favorite food, and that song he loved. Mourning the favorite toy, the friend next door, that familiar blanket. Everything was gone. His entire world was forever altered.

Snuggled closely between us, Lian sobbed, grieving as only a two-year-old knows how, and I gently sang "Jesus Loves Me" as the tears rolled down my cheeks, my heart breaking over his unfathomable loss.

"Little ones to Him belong, they are weak, but He is strong."

I was too choked up to sing. Chris took over, and we joined with our son in his tears. We mourned the loss of his biological family, the loss of his foster mother, the tearing apart that is the life of the orphan. We knew that while we traveled down the road of mourning, we would also eventually arrive at the God-ordained healing of his sweet life. Lian had endured more loss in his almost three years on earth than any of us had endured in a lifetime.

All that day, Lian wept off and on. We sang "You Are My Sunshine," we rocked him, stroked his sweet, soft cheeks, and snuggled him, but we let him cry. These tears were necessary for healing, both for him and for us. Our hearts ached for him. I despised this world. I hated the fact that parents sometimes don't have any choice but to leave their children. I despaired in the fact that orphanages have to exist, that there are so many orphans, that children have to learn to cry, learn to love, learn to **feel**, learn to trust all over again.

And yet, there's this God who sets the solitary in families, and wasn't that what He was doing? Lian was here, sobbing in our arms, and we could willingly take his pain onto our solid shoulders, helping him bear the burden, easing his pain and turning it into joy.

What an incredible privilege this is! What a humbling opportunity to be entrusted with this beautiful little soul who is so undeniably precious in God's sight. Not only did He miraculously bring a family to Lian from halfway across the world, but He also planned that Lian would irrevocably alter our hearts and lives, and the ripple effects of his little life would reach far and wide.

That day of mourning with Lian has forever altered me. It broke me and helped me to comprehend God's heart for orphans and His sacrifice like nothing else ever could.

After that day, there were no more tears. A peace came over Lian that could only be from God. I knew friends and family were praying for us. God heard!

Slowly, slowly, this little one opened up his rosebud heart to us, petal by soft petal. His sweet smile appeared more and more often, at times with a mischievous twinkle in his eye, if he was in the plotting mood.

Homeward bound at last, we found ourselves hurrying through the Raleigh airport, aching to see and hold our three kids. Lian on my hip, the tears started streaming down my face the instant we stepped off the plane. We were home. Lian was an American citizen, a part of our family, and we were all to be united soon. It was an overwhelming, blessed, joyful feeling, and what a beautiful reunion it was! Family, friends, and my youngest were jumping the security line to get to us. (Thank goodness for gracious security guards!)

What a wonderful, balloon-filled flurry of welcome through the haze of utter exhaustion and jet lag! Settling in, we were all so absolutely in love with Lian. Every day was an adventure in bonding, learning to love, and opening up to trust, but I was concerned again.

He didn't cry. Ever. After that one sad day in China, Lian hadn't cried. Even if he accidentally hurt himself, he would stoically endure it with nary a tear.

One evening, Lian discovered he could do somersaults and, *blip*, he flipped over, banging his forehead hard on the corner of the wall. An immediate goose egg appeared, but he didn't cry. He tried to grab the pain with his hand and push it off his head. No tears.

Three months later, there were still no tears. In speaking with the agency's family counselor, I mentioned my concern to her.

"Not good," she stated. "He needs to feel safe enough to cry, to show his emotions to you. You need to get him to cry."

Well now, that was a funny thing to be working on, but here I was, anxiously hoping that he'd cry sometime. Not that I was actively trying to **make** him cry, but I was praying that our bonding and attachment would culminate in a feeling of security for him, a knowledge that we were his parents, and that he was safe with us.

Lian was going through the normal three-year-old stage, and one day he needed a little time out. I sat him down on the floor and said, "You're going to have to sit there for a minute since you did _____."

Suddenly, out of nowhere, the bottom lip trembled, tears welled up, and a small wail erupted from this unhappy little person.

I rushed to him, overjoyed. "Oh, sweetie, good job… I mean, no… Yes, you can cry, good job… but… you need to stay… Oh, forget it."

I scooped him up, and we had a good snuggle. To hear him cry was like music to my soul. He trusted us! Such a strange thing to be worried about, but then again, everything about this child was foreign.

All of my many years of mothering have been scrapped and I am starting over, doing the best I know how, because things are different with Lian. We have to parent him differently than our biological kids. So, we ask God for guidance, read a ton of books and materials, and move forward in the confidence that this is the best we can do.

I am truly astounded at how quickly Lian understood what we were saying to him in English. Within a few short weeks, he would follow simple requests, nod "Yes" or "No," and seemed to be perfectly comfortable with the new language.

Speaking has been a struggle, though. After nineteen months at home, we are still very behind, but on the flip side, we have learned sign language! What a joy it has been, with Lian learning how to sign for everything he needs and all of us having the privilege of learning a brand new language!

I'll end our story with one more anecdote. Long before we started the adoption process, I used to listen to "A Thousand Years" by Christina Perry. You've probably heard the song.

The chorus always squeezed my heart so hard that my eyes would leak.

This song would come on in the car, and every time, it got me. I had waited so very long for this moment. It seemed like a thousand years. I was scared, but so very ready.

Then, we were adopting, and I'd still listen to this song and it would still make me cry.

We discovered—on YouTube—the carpool karaoke song of Mamas and their beautiful kiddos with T21[*] signing that song. Lian LOVES that song now. He watches it every day, he knows all the signs, and we listen to it in the car.

And yes, before bed, that's the song I sing to him almost every night as he drowsily signs it, stars shining on his ceiling, his wave sound maker lightly playing. I gently rub his head as he drifts off.

I have died every day waiting for you… don't be afraid; I have loved you for a thousand years… I'll love you for a thousand more.

Lian – God Has Answered. Alexander – Leader Of Men, Driver.

You're home.

---

[*] Trisomy 21

CHAPTER
THREE

photo © Jamie McDonald Photography

eDie'S story

My husband, Jade, and I are high school sweethearts and well before we ever said, "I do," we had a vision for what our life would look like. Our first daughter, Aubrie, was born in 2005, and our son, Everett, followed in 2007.

We were sitting by a campfire at a friend's thirtieth birthday party when his aunt and uncle walked up with their adult daughter who had Down syndrome. At that moment, I told myself, "I could never do that." I'm pretty sure God had a huge laugh that day, because His plans for our family were vastly bigger and much different then we could have ever imagined. Less than two years from that date, we welcomed our third child, Ollie Faith, complete with designer genes.

Our third pregnancy was routine until our twenty-week ultrasound, at which time we received a prenatal diagnosis of Down syndrome and an AV canal heart defect (which would require open heart surgery). I spent the rest of my pregnancy terrified of her diagnosis and of how it would impact our future and our family. I kept that night by the campfire on repeat over and over in my head. At the time, I was so confused as to why God would lead us down this path. I prayed and prayed that He would take this diagnosis away from her and that we would deliver a child without an extra chromosome.

The moment Ollie was delivered in February of 2011, I saw her face and knew the diagnosis was 100 percent correct. She had Down syndrome. One hot tear slipped down my face in short-lived sadness. The nurses took her from my arms and placed her in her warming basket. I looked over and saw her clutching Jade's finger with a huge smile on her face. Yes, I know babies don't smile intentionally, but I swear that day she did. From that moment forward, I knew our life would be more than okay; it would be great!

I fell head-over-heels in love with our sweet baby girl. She transformed our entire family! My husband, our two other children, and every single person that is involved in Ollie's life are better because they know her and the joy she spreads. It is contagious! I quickly started recognizing Ollie's life as the gift it truly was and started wishing that we could someday have another child with designer genes just like her. They say hindsight is 20/20, and today I can clearly see how wrong I was to fear Down syndrome; God was giving our family a tremendous gift. We wouldn't change a thing about Ollie even if we could.

It was not long after Ollie's birth that our family started reading blogs, watching videos, and becoming familiar with the Reece's Rainbow community. We learned about what happens to children with Down syndrome in other countries, and the stories shattered our hearts.

At the time, we were not in a financial position to move forward with an adoption, but I started praying that one day we could give an orphan a loving home. For over five years I prayed that prayer. Our children were always involved in the dialogue. They would pray for kids, ask about families that were adopting, and practically beg us to bring a child into our family. Despite my desire and his support for other families on the journey, Jade expressed a hard "No" for growing our family beyond three children.

Jade built our dream home on our family's cattle farm during my second pregnancy, and we moved in shortly after Everett's birth. Life was perfect before Ollie came along.

After Ollie's birth, it felt as though everything crashed and burned around us. We blew through our savings as I stayed home to nurse her through heart failure. Then I quit my job to be home with her full-time. What had been our "dream life" suddenly became so incredibly hard, both emotionally and financially.

At four months of age, we handed her over for open-heart surgery. It was the hardest thing we had ever done, and in those moments I pleaded with God to give me a future with this child. God performed a miracle that day through the surgeon's hands. Ollie recovered beautifully and was home within five days with a healthy, functioning heart!

Fast-forward three years, and Jade's company was busy and growing every day. God had led me to an online company where work meant I could change lives and stay home with my kids, all while earning a great income. Our finances had been totally transformed. We were now finally in a position to fund an adoption, but Jade's biggest fear was that we might end up going down that path of financial hardship again. He was happy with our life and terrified that an adoption would damage our family in one way or another. I understood his thought process, but in my heart, I knew we were strong enough in every way to provide for an orphan. In the end, I accepted his position (albeit temporarily), and I just kept praying that one day that door would open for us.

In December of 2014, we had a surprise pregnancy. My husband and I were so excited about a fourth child. Just six weeks into the pregnancy, I had a day that I felt "off." I decided to tell my mom and sisters about the pregnancy earlier than I typically would have, because I was afraid I might miscarry. I asked them to pray for the baby and for me. A few hours later, I woke up in an ambulance with internal bleeding, requiring emergency surgery. It turned out the pregnancy was ectopic, and my fallopian tube had ruptured. We lost the baby.

To say I was devastated is an understatement. I had been ecstatic about this baby, and I felt robbed. I felt as though the baby was gone before we even had a chance to wrap our heads around the idea of it being here. I was shattered. We had already fought our way through so much, and yet here we were again. I tried to make sense of it and, over time, came to believe that our loss was to open our hearts to the possibility of another child. More and more I felt adoption was the way we should go, but Jade stood stoically in his position that our family was complete.

The next two years were incredibly difficult for me. I prayed for my husband, but, if I'm being 100 percent honest, I probably prayed "against" my husband, asking God to change his heart the way I wanted it changed. I prayed that Jade would find himself broken by the plight of these kids, that he would realize the room we had in our hearts and home for another child, that he would say "Yes" to adoption. Meanwhile, I joined Facebook groups that advocated for orphans with Down syndrome. I poured my heart and any extra finances I could into supporting other families that were adopting.

In the spring of 2016, we were invited to a gala that was raising funds to build a home for orphans in Haiti. I thought, "This is it! This is where Jade will finally see my vision of what our family can do for another child." I was so wrong. That gala just exasperated the issues for us. He was being cautious for our family, and I was pushy and angry in response to his decisions. This eventually led us to a meeting with our associate pastor and his wife. I wholeheartedly trusted their guidance. They had adopted twin girls, so they tried their best to be unbiased and to see his perspective. We left their house that day still in disagreement, but we both left with words from our pastor that we could cling to in our marriage.

I can honestly say this was one of the hardest periods of my life. I felt so strongly that God was revealing our family's next path. For the sake of our marriage and our family, I had to choose to stop talking about adoption and turn all the frustration, struggle, and uncertainty over to God in prayer. If I can assure anyone reading this of just one thing, let it be this; prayer is transformative! It was about one month later that Jade said we could move forward in adoption!

I was thrilled, but also fearful that he was only doing this for me and not because he had felt the calling as well. *What if this ruins our marriage? What if this ruins our family? What if I was just imagining that adoption was God's plan for our family? What if this is my selfish need after our ectopic pregnancy?* I kept running those questions through my mind. Then I would pray, and God would remind me that my husband had said, "Yes." That, in and of itself, was a miracle! I gave up my insecurity, and from then on I clung to my faith and my belief that the rest of our journey would fall into place as well.

After Jade agreed, we started looking at adoption websites. It was overwhelming. So many beautiful children were waiting. We sat in my office together one night, scrolling through page after page of profiles. That evening, Jade finally realized how big the need for adoption was.

Just a few days later, I was on Facebook, reading posts in a Down syndrome adoption group, and saw a picture of a beautiful two-year-old girl in China. She had the cutest bob haircut, with thick black bangs. Then I scrolled down and saw a video of her. I pressed play and watched as she "spider monkey" hugged her nanny, wrapping both legs around the nanny's waist. Ollie does the exact same thing! At that moment, hot tears filled my eyes because I **knew** she was our daughter. I showed Jade that night, and he agreed; she was **ours!**

The next day, we sat down with Aubrie and Everett to answer their questions about us moving forward with the adoption. They were completely beside themselves. They both cried and were so excited that they would be getting a second little sister! I immediately reached out to the agency with which that little girl was listed. Since we were starting at ground zero, we had no home study. We had nothing prepared and had a mountain of work ahead of us.

It was a monumental paper chase. Within six days, China had agreed to give us pre-authorization to adopt her. We would name her Edie Joy: "Edie," after her great-grandmother Ethel Edith, and "Joy," because that's what we saw and felt when we watched her videos.

The paperwork felt like the easy part to us, but the emotional weight was incredibly difficult to handle. I think adoption is eerily similar to pregnancy, but more intense. I couldn't sleep, and worried about that little girl every single day. I would pray for her protection, that she was being fed, and that she was not mistreated. I was so eager to get her home, and dreamt about how her body would feel in my arms, the texture of her hair, and what her voice would sound like. I couldn't wait to add her to our family!

Many parents call it "ransoming" your child, and that's exactly how it feels. You feel as though your child is kidnapped halfway around the world and you are racing to get them home as soon as you can. Every step that I could rush along, I did. It was an intense period of faith growth for me because I knew **His** hand was over us and everything would all happen in **His** timing.

We were told it would take a year, but seven months after we started the process, we got the final approval from China that we could travel.

On March 1, 2017, Jade and I hopped on a plane to Beijing. We couldn't wait to finally meet our daughter. We landed in Beijing and thanked the Lord that our guide was there to meet us. She took us to our hotel, and we settled into the reality that we were in China. We had barely slept on the plane; it was 6:00 pm in Beijing but felt more like 6:00 am for us. We grabbed a quick shower to wash off the long flight and went out for dinner.

The next day and a half were spent touring Beijing. As we adjusted to the time difference, we learned about life in China. We wanted to gain an understanding of Edie's culture, to one day be able to share with her our experiences in her country and the love we had for her homeland. I'm forever grateful we had those few days in Beijing to *really* understand where our daughter is from. As we toured, locals were snapping photos of us like paparazzi might. It was one of the wildest adventures we have ever been on!

On Saturday afternoon, we boarded a bullet train to Jinan, Shandong. We would soon be forty-five minutes away from our daughter. We had such eager anticipation mixed with some fear, too. Our child was so close to us and was unknowingly preparing for her last night in her orphanage.

We arrived in Jinan after dark and started the short trip to our hotel. I distinctly remember that while we were driving, it felt as though we had journeyed into a no-mans-land in the middle of a massive city. The city was lit up like Las Vegas, with neon lights juxtaposed against huge skyscrapers that were pitch black and vacant, prepared for the massive population growth that was to come. At one point Jade looked at me and said, "Where did you take us?" The drive that night was an experience we will never forget.

We settled into our hotel quickly, but I don't think I slept a wink that night. I kept picturing Edie. It was her last night in the only home she had ever known. It was her last night immersed in her culture, her food, and her language. It was her last night with the nanny she had known since birth. Tomorrow her whole world would be turned upside down. So many prayers were spoken over her that night. We knew the adjustment for her would be unimaginable!

The wait the next day felt like an eternity. Finally, there was a knock on the door. In walked our guide with the orphanage director and our daughter and her nanny. My heart was leaping out of my chest. I so badly wanted to hold her in my arms, kiss her cheeks, and feel the texture of her hair. I wanted her to know how much she was loved and adored. I wanted to tell her about her family back home that could not wait to meet her. I wanted her to giggle and laugh and to call me "Mama." I had been feeling all those things from the moment I saw her seven months ago, and yet to her, I was a complete stranger that looked like no one she had ever seen before.

We could tell immediately that she was very attached to her nanny and absolutely terrified of us. We would try to interact with her, but she would just cling to her nanny with all that she had. It was so hard to watch her be so scared and uncertain of us, and as much as I wanted to hold and comfort her, I knew it was best to give her time to decide to trust us. Edie had been with the nanny her entire life. The nanny gifted us photos of Edie, from the moment she entered the orphanage until her last day there. There were also video clips of Edie's life and milestones, along with a stack of papers that had photos, and milestones written on the bottom of them.

It was the most beautiful gift; we now have a piece of Edie's past to share with her one day, and we cried alongside the nanny as she said goodbye. Edie was so well loved by that nanny, and we are forever grateful to her for her care of our daughter. The director and the nanny left in less than twenty minutes.

The rest of the day was heartbreaking. Edie was terrified. Everything and everyone she had known was taken from her. All of her comfort in this world was gone. Silent tears rolled down her face; she did not make a sound as she cried. We could hold her, but she wouldn't eat or drink, and lay limp and defeated on our shoulders. After a while, she finally fell asleep on my chest. I watched her sleep (which I had waited for so long to do!) and prayed that she would soon start to trust us, because we would never abandon her.

I think Jade cried just as much as Edie that day. In the back of my mind, I had still been so worried that perhaps he wasn't "all in" on this adoption. I had worried for months that he did it for me and that he wouldn't feel a connection and bond with this new little girl. That day, as I watched him be overwhelmed with empathy and love, I knew he was all in. He was heartbroken for her, and in love with his new daughter. He told me later that the moment Edie walked into the room, he felt the same emotions he had experienced when our biological children were delivered. She was ours. We immediately bonded with her, but it would take time for her to bond with us.

The next day we went to finalize the adoption and apply for her passport. It was the hardest day so far because all you really want to do is stay in your room and get to know your child, but you can't. Throughout the day Edie was very sad, very quiet, and very shy. She would barely move, and spent the day sitting on our lap and napping a lot. I remember us just staring at her in awe and love. That day she officially became a Reid but, as exciting as that was, watching her grieve so deeply made it an equally sad day as well.

After a long day of traveling to finalize the adoption and get Edie's passport, we were back in the hotel. This was the time we needed to get to know our daughter. We planned to play any kind of game that would promote bonding and attachment. She loved stacking cups, and by the end of the night, she would knock them over and laugh so hard! That was the very first time we saw our daughter smile or even interact with us. We shed many happy tears seeing our sweet girl opening up. It was everything we had been praying for.

Each day we spent with her, her shell would open up just a

little bit more. When we were in our hotel room, we would watch her giggling and playing. In those moments we could feel her starting to love us, and that was priceless and full of hope! Then, as soon as we would step out of the room, she would withdraw and become quiet again.

There was so much hope in our hearts in this part of the process. We were anxious for her to adore us and for us to experience her true personality, but we knew it would take patience and time for that trust to develop. So each day we just poured our hearts into hers, showing her with our actions that we were always going to be there for her.

The week we spent in her capital city was our favorite. There were canals lined with weeping willows where people gathered at the natural springs to get water. Everywhere there were elderly men on the sidewalk playing checkers, or women line dancing in groups in the park. We walked through streets filled with all kinds of Chinese food. The city square was full of people flying kites, and old men dancing with chain whips; their *pop pop* filled the air, and men on roller skates hit tops with whips to keep them spinning. It was fascinating to see how they would gather to exercise and engage in hobbies that are vastly different from what we enjoy at home. We fell in love with Edie's capital city and took many photos and videos to share with her one day.

After eighteen days in China, we boarded a plane to fly home to America. We landed in Chicago and were in tears as we anxiously awaited the immigration process that would officially make her a U.S. citizen. We knew her life would forever be changed by the title, "American," and the privileges she would now receive were too many to count.

In China, she would have aged out of her orphanage at age fourteen, and from that point on, her future would have been grim. In America, she is attending school with typical peers. She can graduate high school and college. She can find meaningful, gainful employment; she adds value to our community. Walking through those airport doors and onto American soil gave our daughter a future she could never have found in her home country.

After the long flight and the process of leaving the airport, we settled into the last leg of our trip, a four-hour drive home. We were so excited to see our children and to introduce Edie to them and the rest of our family. We walked in the door to posters and signs and to our kids, who were ecstatic for us to finally be home. It felt so good to be reunited!

Edie was instantly overwhelmed and cried the moment we got home. Everything was still a new experience for her. She was walking into a house with people that loved her and called her sister and granddaughter, but they were strangers to her. That first night of having us all under the same roof was the best night of sleep I had in years because I knew we were complete and whole. My heart was full of joy, and there was no more wondering about my daughter halfway around the world. She was finally home.

That night everyone went to bed, and we looked forward to the next day of bonding. We played all day, and while by the end of the day Edie was not yet comfortable, she was a lot less scared. Every day after that got better. She would allow my mom to visit and to sit by her on the floor; when she had had enough, she would scoot away. Even though she wasn't verbal yet, her body language made her feelings very obvious. Eventually, she started sitting with Ollie and playing with her toys. She would give Everett hugs and kisses and get him to make her laugh. Then, she would seek out Aubrie any time she left the room. She was bonding with the entire family and adjusting beautifully to being a Reid.

Watching her bond and attach to our family would provoke moments of tears for me. I had prayed for her for so many months and worried about how she would adjust to home and all the changes in her life. Seeing her adapting and growing was pure joy to a mama's heart.

As the days pass by, we continue to see who Edie is as a person and are witnessing her growing out of her shell. She has absolutely thrived with the love of a family. Today, Edie Joy is such a different child than the one we met in China; confident and highly independent, super smart, and very opinionated. She has a great sense of humor, too! She is blooming in preschool and is well adjusted, attached, and fiercely bonded to us, an absolute light to our family, and such a gift!

The joy of adoption is not singular. I see it every day, in the minutia of our lives. It's something as simple as watching her walk over to the play set or trampoline in the backyard to play with her siblings. It's watching her giggle with her Daddy. It's her waking up in the morning and climbing into our bed to cuddle. It's in the moments when she searches out her older siblings at a sporting event and yells their names, waving, with a huge grin on her face. It fills my heart to overflowing on the days that we pull into Grandma and Grandpa's driveway and she starts cheering and clapping. It's watching her as she prays with Ollie at bedtime and the dinner table. Adoption is redemption for Edie. One year later, every single day, there are moments where I watch her and think, *Praise Jesus that she is ours, and that we didn't miss this.*

We look at Edie daily and are still in awe of the adoption process. We feel beyond privileged to be her parents. We are so grateful that God called us to this journey, and that we were able to say "Yes." Edie is as much a Reid as our biological children, and we cannot even fathom what our life would look like without her. She is Ollie's best friend, and when we look at their future, we can't wait to see what they accomplish, hand in hand, because both now have a buddy to experience life with.

Adoption is the most bittersweet gift we have ever received. In our greatest joys, there is sorrow at the loss that both Edie and her birth family had to endure. Her family had to say "No" to her, for us to say "Yes." There is heartache alongside incredible happiness. There are two families forever woven together to create the tapestry of Edie's life. We are forever grateful to her biological parents for giving her this future and allowing her to be deeply loved by us. Their sacrifice is never taken lightly, because we know how hard that choice had to have been. Both families had, and still have, one goal in mind; to give Edie the best life possible.

I only wish her birth parents knew how beautiful Edie's life is today. They would be so thrilled for her. I pray for them often, that they innately know that she is adored and thriving. I pray they know that their hardest choice has turned into something beautiful for their Sun An Xiu, our Edie Joy Reid.

CHAPTER
FOUR

penelope's story

Adoption has been engraved on my heart since I was a little girl playing with baby dolls. I can vividly remember standing in a toy aisle and choosing a doll that I was going to pretend I had adopted from Africa. That sweet little doll holds the first memory I have of my desire to adopt. It was a desire that continued to grow as I did, and was fueled even more when I watched my aunt and uncle adopt my cousin from China.

By the time I reached college, I was confident that this longing was a calling from God. When I heard verses like James 1:27a, "Pure and genuine religion in the sight of God the Father means caring for orphans and widows in their distress," I could so clearly feel the Holy Spirit nudging my heart. Choosing to bring a baby into my home was the way I was going to be obedient to this command.

When my husband, Jason, and I started dating, I was quick to tell him of these plans for the future. Even though he didn't share my passion, he said it was something he could get on board with down the road. I knew a decision this life-changing wasn't something he should merely support; he needed to feel God was calling him to it. It wasn't my job to talk him into it. I became quiet about the topic and began to pray.

Jason and I had been married for about two years when our precious baby boy, Parker, was born. We were instantly overcome with love for this little guy, and this love was fierce, humbling, and like nothing we had ever experienced before. Knowing there were children across the world who didn't have anyone to love them in this way put a deep ache within my soul.

My longing to adopt became even stronger, and I started praying more fervently for God to speak to Jason. Sure enough, just a few months later, our church had a special night centered on adoption. After the service, Jason told me that he felt the Holy Spirit put adoption on his heart; he not only felt called to do it, but he wanted to pursue it soon. I am pretty sure I started Googling adoption agencies about five minutes after our conversation. I was beyond thrilled, and it was beautiful to witness the power of prayer so tangibly.

We spent the next few months meeting with people who had gone through the adoption journey, and spent hours upon hours researching. Through this, we found that most of the countries in which we were interested required couples to have been married for five years and be at least thirty years of age. We met none of these requirements. We were pretty bummed about this information, but we used this time of waiting to start fundraising.

We also began praying that God would give us some clarity of which country to choose. I was hoping for some writing on the wall, or for Jason and I to both have the same amazing dream that would clearly tell us where our child was waiting for us. Instead, we simply felt a quiet nudge toward China. There was never a point when we were absolutely certain that it was the right choice, but we knew there was a need there, and we had peace in our hearts to continue in that direction unless God closed the door.

We also had another baby during this time of waiting, a beautiful little girl we named Paisley Jane. She was born right after my twenty-ninth birthday; we could now officially start our paperwork because we were just one year shy of being able to send it to China.

The mountains of paperwork and the interviews were going smoothly until we got to the special needs checklist. This form had hundreds of different medical conditions on it, and we had to go through each one of them and check, "Would consider," or, "Would not consider." It was overwhelming, to say the least, and not just because we couldn't even pronounce half of them and had no idea what they entailed, but because we knew there were children out there that had these conditions. Checking "Would not consider" was saying "No" to a child who desperately needed a mom and dad. It felt selfish and awful, and it was so hard to get through.

But when we got to the Down syndrome checkbox, our decision came without too much struggle. It's difficult to admit, but Down syndrome—or any other kind of cognitive delay—had always been a fear of mine. It was something I specifically prayed against when we were expecting both of our babies, and brought me anxiety until we reached that twenty-week ultrasound. There wasn't any part of me that felt called to adopt a child with Down syndrome. So we took our pen and quickly checked "Would not consider."

Our dossier was done, and all we had to do was wait until my birthday to mail it. During this last month of waiting, I had a friend tell me there was a podcast I needed to hear. She had just listened to it and felt God calling her to tell me about it. A few days later, I had a different friend also tell me about a podcast I needed to listen to. Knowing how God works, I am sure it comes as no surprise when I say that it was the same podcast my first friend had mentioned. I decided it must be pretty good, so I took the time to listen to it.

The podcast featured an interview with a woman named Heather Avis who was an adoptive mom of three, two of whom had Down syndrome. I was confused as to why two of my friends would think I needed to hear this. Sure, it was about adoption, but the main focus was about adopting a child with Down syndrome. That wasn't going to be my story. At any rate, the podcast was very moving, and I remember thinking to myself, *I am so thankful there are women like Heather that say "Yes" to that calling, because I would never be one of them.*

I went to sleep later that night thinking about the podcast. I woke up the next morning thinking about the podcast, and whenever I had a quiet moment, quotes from the podcast were on repeat in my head. Surely it would stop consuming me in a couple of weeks. However, weeks went by, and I still couldn't get it off my heart. We had completed our adoption process and sent our dossier to China. All we had to do was wait for God to match us with the child He had for us, but why on earth could I not stop thinking about adopting a child with Down syndrome?

I hadn't shared any of what was going on in my heart with Jason, but I decided to casually ask him if he would ever consider adopting a child with Down syndrome. Without hesitating for a second, he said, "Yes." I couldn't deny the feeling that God was starting something, but I tried to convince myself that He was just preparing us for how He would use us in the special needs community in the future. It wasn't about adoption. I did my best to push all these feelings aside, and Jason and I had no further conversation about it.

A few weeks later we were out to eat with some friends, chatting about nothing important, when Jason looked at me and asked, "Would you consider changing our paperwork to say it's okay if our little girl has Down syndrome?" I laughed nervously and said, "Whoa, that is a serious question for taco Tuesday!" Seeing he was serious, I immediately started listing all my fears. "So you're okay if we are never empty nesters? Who is going to take care of her when we die? What if something is wrong with her heart?"

I had wanted to adopt since I was a little girl, but this was not what I had pictured. This was not what I wanted. Why was he bringing this up? But I had an undeniable sense that everything God had been doing in my heart was preparing me for this question. We had no idea what our next step should be, so Jason and I both agreed to start by reading the book, *The Lucky Few*, by Heather Avis, the lady who was interviewed in the podcast to which I had listened.

The next night we were at church, worshipping with the youth group and singing the song, "Oceans." As I was singing the words, "Spirit lead me where my trust is without borders, let me walk upon the waters, wherever you would call me," tears immediately welled up in my eyes, and I had to stop singing. I didn't mean those words, and as silly as it sounds, I didn't want God to hear me saying them. I didn't want to be in a place where my trust was without borders, because I knew exactly what those borders were. I could feel the Holy Spirit calling us to say "Yes" to adopting a child with Down syndrome. Fear overwhelmed my heart, and my future felt blurry.

Jason came home from work the next day with *The Lucky Few.* I immediately started reading it, and was convicted by every page. I read Heather's words, "I wonder how many times we, His children, choose a comfortable no over a terrifying yes - the kind of yes that will lead us to the only place we should ever long to be: in the arms of Jesus," and it was as though she had looked into my heart and was talking just to me. For months I had been convicted of my desire to simply live a life that was comfortable. I didn't want to be stretched or challenged, and I thought my willingness to adopt should be enough. It's hard to admit, but I was upset with God for asking me to take it a step further and say "Yes" to something that scared me so much.

At the end of this crazy week, I texted some of my closest friends and told them what was going on. I asked when they could come over, in hopes they would justify my fears and tell me I couldn't handle this. One of them contacted me separately a few minutes later. She knew a girl from high school that had adopted a little girl with Down syndrome from China just a few weeks ago. (Okay God, I get it.) As I was scrolling through this girl's pictures of their trip to China, I felt, for the first time, a peace that passed my understanding. I was overcome with excitement that this could also be our future, and my fear turned into an unexplainable joy!

I wish I could say that from this moment on it was smooth sailing and the fear completely disappeared, but Jason and I both struggled with doubt. This decision was going to affect the rest of our lives. What if we regretted it? But during this season between doubt and certainty, a little girl named Mandy kept popping up in my head. Weeks earlier, I had seen her on our agency's Facebook group of waiting children. She was darling, and I had clicked on her picture, but the moment I read "Down syndrome" in her description, I quickly exited and kept scrolling.

Now that we were genuinely considering this, I couldn't get that precious little girl out of my head. I showed Jason her picture. He said he had also seen her on Facebook and thought it wouldn't hurt to ask if her file was still available. Sure enough, it was, but only for another two weeks. Our agency had had her file for so long—without anyone showing any interest—that if a family didn't decide to adopt her within the next two weeks, she would be put back on the shared list. Two weeks? We hadn't even officially decided that we were going to adopt a child with Down syndrome.

Even though we had some undeniable confirmation, we needed to pray and be certain about it for at least a couple of months, right? There was no way we could decide about this little girl in just fourteen days. Then we watched the video of her, and everything changed. Her smile, her wobbly little walk, the look of pride in her deep eyes when she completed the ring tower on which she was working; there was something about her that just felt like she was ours. We took that first step of faith and put her file on hold. We now had seven days to make a decision that would forever affect our lives and the life of a precious little girl across the globe.

We talked to as many trusted families as we could, sent her file to our doctor and, of course, begged God to give us clear direction. Somewhere in the midst of this week, Jason and I both knew that adopting a child with Down syndrome was something we were being called to, but was Mandy "the one"? Was she the child about which I had been praying and dreaming since I was a little girl? We really felt as though she could be, but there just wasn't that certainty that I had read about in so many blogs, where the parents saw the picture and just knew. Plus, it didn't seem wise to say "Yes" to the first file we looked at.

We started looking at other available children, and after scrolling through about six pages of pictures, there she was again; our Mandy. We wanted her to be our daughter. Even so, we struggled with uncertainty, but she was a healthy two-year-old who needed a mom and dad to love her, so we took that second step of faith and said "Yes" to pursuing Mandy. We named her Penelope Joy.

The process went smoothly, and before we knew it, we had our Letter of Approval from China. Our caseworker said that if everything went as it should, we would be traveling to China in about six months. My suitcase was already open on my bedroom floor, ready to go, so I did not appreciate this timeline. The idea of waiting even a week to bring our daughter home felt like torture. She was waiting for us, and I felt an urgency in my heart to bring her home that consumed my every thought.

I did my best to trust in God's perfect timing while also asking Him to let it be sooner than expected. He was so sweet to answer this prayer. Steps that were supposed to take at least two weeks took less than twenty-four hours, and only four months into our six-month wait, our agency called and asked if we could have our "gotcha" day in just a week-and-a-half. We finished packing (which took me five minutes, since I had started four months ago), made all our arrangements, and traveled to Houston to get our visas.

That last week was a roller coaster of emotion. The consulate ended up denying our visas—because Jason is a minister—just three days before we were supposed to get on the plane to China. Our flights and hotel were booked, and Penny's orphanage had been told we were coming. The situation was out of our hands, so again we prayed, and just as we had seen time and time again throughout this adoption journey, God made a way! The consulate released our visas on Friday morning, so my dad got on a plane and brought them to us—since we lived eight hours away—and our flight left at five o'clock that afternoon. Sitting on that plane on our way to get our beloved daughter felt like a dream.

A day of travel and one day of rest later, it was finally time to meet our Penelope Joy. Our agency had done their best to prepare us for the realities of "gotcha" day. It was going to be in a hot government building, there were going to be tons of other families there, it was going to be fast, and there were probably going to be a lot of screaming kids. Even though the majority of that was true, it was still just beautiful to us.

We arrived at 2:00 pm, were shuffled to a couch, and were surrounded by other nervous families. Names were called one by one, and it was such an incredible joy to witness other families have their babies placed in their arms. The tears started flowing long before we even saw our Penelope.

The minutes felt like hours as we waited, but, finally, our guide called our name. Jason and I hurried to the other side of the room, handed off our phones for people to take pictures, and held our breath. She stepped out of the curtain walking hand-in-hand with two of her nannies, and we dropped to our knees and watched her walk toward us. Everything else in the noisy room disappeared, and it was as if it was just her and us.

Absolute joy overwhelmed our hearts as we watched her wobble toward us, but the reality of what was happening in her life at this moment was not lost on us. She had already lost her mom and dad, and now she was losing the nannies who she knew as her mommas. She was being handed to strangers who didn't look or sound like her. We knew she was scared, but still, she so bravely walked straight into our arms! It was a holy moment, and gave us such a beautiful image of Jesus and His work of redemption in our lives.

Our first twenty-four hours with her were amazing, over-whelming, happy, and also really nerve-wracking. Our sweet girl was frozen. She had zero expression and showed no signs of emotion, not even one tear. She wouldn't budge, and when we tried to move her arms or legs, she would hold them in the exact spot to which we moved them. We honestly didn't know if she was petrified, or if she had been in the orphanage so long that she didn't know how to convey emotion.

It was scary for us, and that first night with her wasn't how I always imagined it would be. It was hard. I had dreamed for so long of being able to rock her to sleep, and here she was, and I didn't feel as I thought I should. She felt like a stranger in my arms, and I hated it. I had anticipated not feeling an instant connection, and knew the bonding process would take time, but it still over-whelmed my heart with guilt.

The next morning and afternoon, Penelope was still stoic, with no expression or independent movement, until we got out the stickers. I handed her one, which she took and put on her forehead. Her whole face lit up, and her mouth formed the most breathtaking smile. We were overjoyed, and I felt an immediate weight come off my chest.

It didn't take long after that for her to come completely out of her shell, and she had us chasing her giggly self around the hotel room. Our two weeks with her in China now hold some of our dearest memories. It was such a sweet time for the three of us, but by the end of it, we were definitely ready to go home and start our life as a family of five.

I was anticipating a hard adjustment period after we got home, but everything went smoothly. Our other two children welcomed her with open arms, especially our three-year-old son, who was instantly smitten with her and quickly took on the role of protector.

However, a few days after we settled in, Penelope bit Paisley Jane. My gut response was to yell, "How dare you bite my daughter!" I felt sick that I would even think that; Penelope was my daughter too, but at that point, it still didn't feel that way. The guilt that started that first night in China grew even stronger, and it is something I continue to fight. It is so hard to admit that our love for her is still growing even now, after we have been home a little over a year. I read other adoptive momma's stories, and sometimes get jealous of the ones who say that it was genuine love at first sight with their child.

For us, it is taking time. I think one reason it is so difficult is because our society portrays "love" to be all about feelings and emotions. God has been sweet to remind us that love looks a lot different in the Bible. It is something you choose, and it is an action. It isn't always accompanied by happy and gushy feelings. Don't get me wrong; we do love her and gush over her adorable self, but the deep feelings are not always where we wish they were. It takes a lot more work and intentionality. We know, however, that we are still in the bonding season, and Jason and I wouldn't trade it for anything. We still can't believe God gave us the undeserved gift of being able to raise this precious girl.

Life with our Penelope Joy is truly beautiful. She is tenderhearted, gentle, silly, kind, fun, smart, hard-working, and determined. She has helped us slow down, laugh more, and find joy and excitement in the little things. Her meltdowns are big, but so is her love, and we are thankful for the balance. We know challenges will come, as they do with every child, but we believe we serve a God who is faithful and will give us what we need to see it through. We want to shout from the mountain tops that Penelope is our daughter, perfectly made in the image of God, and we wouldn't take away her Down syndrome even if we could.

There have been a lot of hard things throughout this process, but it doesn't mean it hasn't been good. We would choose to do it all over again in a heartbeat. We both believe she was always meant to be a part of our family, and it still amazes me to think of how God started weaving Penelope's story with ours in a toy aisle across the world from her, twenty-two years before she was born. We can't imagine our lives without her. We are so thankful for how God showed us His story of redemption through our process of finding and bringing her home.

Our journey has taught us so much about the love God has for us as His children. He is such a good father, and it is only by His holy and precious Spirit that we have the hope of doing right by these precious babes that He has entrusted to us! "God sent him to buy freedom for us who were slaves to the law, so that he could adopt us as his very own children. And because we are his children, God has sent the Spirit of his Son into our hearts, prompting us to call out, 'Abba, Father.' Now you are no longer a slave but God's own child" (Galatians 4:5-7 NLT).

CHAPTER
FIVE

eLLiOTT'S story

There we were, sitting at the local Steak & Shake on our very first date, discussing baby names. I (Jay) wanted a daughter named Brooke and a son named Brandon. The tall, slender brunette (Kristin) with a faint sprinkle of freckles with whom I was sharing said date had her boy name, Josiah, picked out.

Why would a young couple, sixteen and seventeen years of age, be talking about baby names on a first date? Who knows... that was just us having an innocent conversation. It was no secret that we both wanted children, and more than just a few, although I have certainly toned it down from wanting ten; I slammed on the brakes at six. Well, we were married three years later, and the babies started coming!

First, there was Anson Joe. Named after both of my grandfathers, he was the first baby born in our county in 2006. A sports fanatic (which I definitely am not) with a competitive spirit (which he gets from both sides of the family), Anson is often in the center of a good-natured but lively debate concerning his favorite basketball player, LeBron something or other.

Then came Faith Alivia. Born in June of 2007 with a perfectly round face, she had me, her daddy, from "hello." A daddy-pleasing, brother-bossing, hard worker when she wants to be, "little mother hen" best describes our Faith. And boy, she's a looker, just like her mom.

In February of 2009, the Lord blessed us with another son we named Noah Carson. With his sparkling eyes and quick wit, Noah is the one who keeps us on our toes and holding our breath whenever we're around other folks. Never one to know a stranger and with curiosity to burn, Noah will often say the first thing that comes to his mind. (Which may or may not come from his Dad's side of the family.)

In October of 2011, Jake Preston was born into our family. Jake's philosophy? It's better to ask forgiveness than permission. Permission, that is, to tear anything and everything apart to build something new, using tools from you-know-who's limited stash. Jake never ceases to amaze us with his unending curiosity and ingenuity.

And then, all of a sudden, Faith had to share that special place reserved in a daddy's heart for daughters. Sarah Kate was born in December of 2013. Named after her daddy's mom and an aunt, Sarah Kate came into our lives bringing with her a little more girl drama, two little dimples, and one more reason her daddy should get himself a shotgun. This little darling is often Jake's partner in crime. She shares his ambition of trying to say the entire alphabet in burps and enjoys playing with toads. What a perfect family, right?

So why, in late fall of 2014, were Kristin and I talking about adopting a child with Down syndrome? We're not sure, except we feel it was definitely a God thing. For as long as I can remember, I had a longing to be around people with Down syndrome. I grew up knowing a handful of them, and as I got older, I realized the traits they shared were ones I wanted for myself. Traits I hoped someday to instill in my children. Love... and I mean real love. The kind that does not envy, or boast, or judge; a real, genuine, compassionate, we're-in-this-thing-together type of love.

Even before we were married, Kristin and I had decided we would not be disappointed should God create one of our children with an extra chromosome. We had never gotten to the point of asking God for a child with Down syndrome, nor had we ever discussed adoption. Why should we have? God was blessing us left and right with healthy children and memories. And oh boy, are there memories! We will save those for a different book with more room.

Our Sarah Kate was not yet a year old when one day we received, in the mail, a publication with an ad from the National Down Syndrome Adoption Network (NDSAN). I clearly remember getting a little warm on the inside and my heart skipping a few beats when I came across the ad. I told God right then and there that I was open to the possibility of adopting a child with Down syndrome. I tend to be pretty frank when having a conversation with God, and I told Him He would have to be the one to tell Kristin if this was something He actually wanted us to pursue. And I left it at that.

The next evening Kristin brought my attention to the ad. She asked me what I thought of checking into it, and that is where the conversation started. We agreed on a few things from the get-go.

First, we would let God know we were serious about being open to adopting a child with Down syndrome, but there would be no disappointment if this thing didn't work out. After all, we thought, we weren't lacking in the children department of our family. We would pursue this thing, but not be forceful along the way. We would be open and willing, should God see us fit to care for one of His dearest.

Second, we would wait a year to apply for adoption. We wanted Sarah Kate to be at least two years old. Third, we didn't want to wait too long to start the process of adoption because we wanted this child to grow up right in the middle of our biological children. If we weren't matched with a child after a year or two, we would simply take our names off the list and call it good. Fourth, this was our decision to make. We needed to be grounded in our decision before telling anyone. We knew from the beginning that we would face at least some opposition from those closest to us.

After three months of praying and talking it over, we knew we wanted to pursue this further. We told both sets of parents first. Then we told others. Opposition did come. We heard all the what-ifs you can think of. What about your other children? Do you realize this child will never move out? What if you don't love him like you love your biological children? Would God not have given you a child with Down syndrome biologically if He had wanted you to have one? The list goes on.

We felt that some of the questions were ridiculous, but honestly, most of the opposition we received was genuine concern about the health and well-being of our existing family of seven. Could we handle the added responsibility? Did we know what we were getting ourselves into? One thing we both knew for sure was that ours was not a perfect family, rather quite dysfunctional at times, and probably, by some standards, not qualified for the job. But we also knew that our home, compared to much of the world, is a stable one.

Our home is filled with forgiveness, love, and laughter, and then forgiveness again, because it takes a lot of that some days. Our home is one where Mom and Dad love each other and are in it for the long haul. We also knew that our child with Down syndrome would receive plenty of stimulation every waking hour from his siblings, which could work as well as professional therapy services.

On the flip side, we felt as though this child could teach us all a thing or two about love. And if God were for this, which we felt He certainly was, would He not see us through? As the word got out about us longing to adopt, we were overwhelmed with support and well wishes, which way overshadowed the naysayers. Our church supported us, which felt good, and we got encouragement from folks we barely knew or didn't know at all. Our children were all agreed that having a sibling with Down syndrome would be cool. The only concern came from Noah, who was worried that his new brother or sister would chew with his or her mouth open.

At the three-month mark, with our decision made to pursue this course, I made the call to the NDSAN. I had to leave a message. The following day, someone returned my call. Phone in hand, I stepped into a back room of the retail grocery store I co-own and manage to speak with a representative about our new adventure. We spoke for almost thirty minutes about the process and the best way to get started. After I hung up, I whispered a tiny prayer of, *Okay, Lord, here goes... show us the way.*

I stepped back out into the retail part of our store, and right smack dab in the middle of my path sat my angel for the day. A young boy with Down syndrome was sitting in a shopping cart, looking straight at me with a huge smile and his arms open wide! He wanted a hug from me. After receiving my hug from heaven, I confided in his mother about the call I had just made. I found out she had adopted not one, but two little angels, and she gave the best encouragement and advice anyone can give. Encouragement and advice derived from experience. This little God wink, as I like to call them, was just the start of many more.

Kristin and I decided to start the process of getting approved to adopt right away. We knew we weren't quite ready to add to our family but wanted to get started so we would be approved for adoption once we were ready. We were told the process could take six months, and once approved, the wait for our match could take years.

We took the required classes, filled out the plethora of paperwork, and had our home studies completed. Our plan was to get approved to adopt and then register with the NDSAN, which had been helping us all along the way. About ten months had passed when, in late December of 2015, we got a call from some friends who just happened to be the owners of the publication in which we first saw the ad from the NDSAN. Marlin and Lisa told us about a boy that was being placed for adoption and gave us the contact information of the agency in charge.

We were about two weeks away from being approved for adoption; was this our first possibility? *Sure, why not inquire?* we thought. Sarah Kate was almost two years old, and we guessed we were probably ready, right? Besides, what were the chances we would be matched with the first child that comes along? Our biggest hold-up, though, was the fact that we were not prepared financially. I called the agency in charge, had a good chat, and was told to call back once we were officially approved. Two weeks later, after being approved, we sent our brand new home study to the agency.

A few days later, we were told they wanted more information on our family. After sending more information, including pictures of our family and notes from all seven of us, we were told that we were one of four families selected for a phone interview. Wow! This was getting exciting. We had been warned by people not to get too excited when a prospect came along. Most people went through many potential prospects before finally being matched. But how could we not get excited? This could be the real deal!

And the real deal it was! Less than two weeks after we were officially approved for adoption, we were told we were the for-ever family chosen for Elliott Joeb. We got to visit him one time before making the twelve-hour one-way trip to bring him home on Mother's Day, 2016.

Elliott has quite the story to tell. He was born in January of 2011 in Bulgaria. His mother dropped him off at an orphanage after finding out he had Down syndrome. When he was four years old, he was adopted to the States, but his second home was not meant to be. We adopted him from his second home and are now his third home, where he will hang out until he reaches his fourth and final home on Heaven's bright shore.

And guess what? Due to the unusual circumstances of Elliott's second adoption, our adoption fees were a fraction of the cost of what we thought they would be. Another one of many God winks! We can honestly say that from day one, Elliott has been just as loved and cherished as any of our biological children.

The very first night when we got home, Elliott marched right up to bed and slept with his brothers all night. He has fit right in with our family from the beginning. It's amazing how many folks think he is one of our biological children, as he does look like his daddy.

We have been pretty fortunate as far as Elliott's health goes. Other than needing custom orthotics to support and correct his ankles and once breaking a leg in a fall, he has not needed any major medical attention. We have learned that, as a good friend told us, there is nothing special about being special. Elliott is expected to behave and conduct himself as independently as reasonably possible. We have found that firm repetition is needed whenever we are teaching him something new, and Kristin is just the woman for the job; don't let her sweet, pretty face fool you. Elliott's stubbornness has met its match, and it is his mom that can get the best results when teaching him something new.

Do we have struggles with Elliott? You'd better believe it, we do. But is it all worth it? And would we do it all over again? Yup, and yup! Our family has been made better and stronger through our adoption of Elliott, and we feel the best is yet to come.

At this time, Elliott says one audible word; "Mom." Otherwise, he is not yet verbal. We are hopeful that someday he will be. And if he never is? We will love him all the same… for who he is. He definitely knows how to get his point across with sign language, facial expressions, and pointing.

His favorite hobbies are listening to me sing, watching his mom sweep or vacuum the floor, listening to anyone read him stories, and sitting beside the leaf blower, waiting for someone to use it. And eating! He loves eating, especially pretzels, and the teachers at his private learning center have capitalized on this inside information. They will reward good behavior by giving him a pretzel and punish bad behavior by taking one away. This method has worked very well, and Elliott excels in his class.

Elliott likes everyone he meets and has a ready smile with tons of energy for anyone interested in playing with him. He can go from zero to sixty in two seconds. He will sit like a perfect gentleman all day in church with his dad, but as soon as church is over, he will be going from person to person looking for a party. He can get fired up really fast and knows who will let him get away with what. Our biological children have grown so much mentally and emotionally since Elliott has joined our family. They all love him to death and show it in their own special ways.

Elliott has learned so much from watching and interacting with his siblings, although sometimes it takes looking back and comparing then to now to realize just how much he has gained. We have made many new friends through the addition of Elliott to our family. We have met many folks who have a family member with Down syndrome, and they have given much great advice.

One thing we were told before we had Elliott was that children with Down syndrome need routine to thrive. This could be a problem, we thought, as routine is not really in our family's vocabulary. We are more of an unrehearsed, game-for-anything, plans-can-change-instantly type of family, and we didn't know how this would all play out for Elliott. But all is good; he has been a real trouper, and he thrives in our family.

We have learned that just like typically developing children, each child with Down syndrome has their own unique personality. We have also noticed that any love that is poured into the heart of a child with Down syndrome will be multiplied and returned in so many ways.

It is important to not limit our son by what we believe he can accomplish, but rather be cheerleaders all along the way so he can be all he can be. We have to take one day at a time when teaching new things, to take the time and teach the same thing over and over again until he gets it, even when it would be so much easier and faster to just do it for him. That advice comes from more than one parent of older children with Down syndrome. Now is the time, when he is young, to teach these things.

We enjoy celebrating each milestone, however big or small, that our son conquers, as he must work harder than most to reach them. Most of the naysayers, even though they gave us their advice and we didn't take it, are now some of our greatest supporters and love Elliott unconditionally.

In addition to getting to know folks who have family members with Down syndrome, we have made lasting friendships with others who have adopted children. We have been asked whether we would encourage other folks to adopt a child with Down syndrome. Our reply is that we would never talk anyone into a decision to adopt, nor condemn anyone who chooses not to. The decision to adopt should be a unanimous one, made by a team of three: God, husband, and wife. But simply put, we sure are glad we did!

I jokingly tell our biological children they are not allowed to date until the age of eighteen but must be out of the house before they turn twenty-one. Guess we nipped that whole idea in the bud when we adopted Elliott, but it's all good. My wife and I look forward to sharing our entire lives with Elliott, even retirement. We think it will be wonderful to hang out with him here on earth and in eternity.

I think back to the day when Kristin and I were sitting in a booth at Steak & Shake. She was eating french fries and a side-by-side (vanilla & chocolate) milkshake. I had my favorite, the Frisco burger. Seventeen years later, and here I sit with a beautiful, loving wife, and six of the finest kids you will ever find... I don't deserve this. Thanks, God; you rock!

CHAPTER

SIX

THE BLENDED BUNCH

Here's the story of a single lady,
who was working hard to pay all of her bills.
She had a small house, a dog and kitty,
and earrings made of pearls.

Here's the story of a dad named Bryan
who was bringing up two cute kids of his own.
They were all there, living in a condo,
yet they were all alone.

Till the one day when the lady met their Daddy,
and they knew it was much more than a hunch.
That our God would somehow form our family;
that's the way we all became the blended bunch.

The Blended Bunch,

The Blended Bunch,

That's the way we became the Blended Bunch!

Okay, that's only part of the story...

My story begins back in 1950 when my Aunt Karen (KK) was born with Down syndrome. I surpassed her in height by the time I was ten. A few short years later, I was "babysitting" her. I adored her. I thought everything she did was cool. Coupon cutting; awesome. Dancing alone in her room, spinning in circles; is there room for one more? Sorting coupons; I'm down. Country music; yeehaw! I went with her to Special Olympics bowling, dances, events, her special church class, and more. I was her biggest fan.

KK worked at the County Board workshop. Sometimes her paychecks were $0.23, but it didn't matter to her. She was thrilled to rip open the envelope and show off the fruits of her labor, waving it in the air as she exited the bus.

My grandmother volunteered at the workshop every Tuesday morning, specifically in the Gift Garden, where artwork was proudly displayed and sold. Though I could barely see over the abnormally tall counter, I tagged along, admiring each artist's labor of love.

Over the years, I volunteered in special education classrooms, babysat kids with special needs, and attempted to help Special Olympians learn to swim. I quickly learned their swimming skills far surpassed mine, so I bailed.

Twenty years ago, as I was walking into my middle school gymnasium, I imagined that I would not *have* babies, but instead, someday, I would *adopt* a baby. A girl! And there it was; my calling to adopt. Nothing fancy or elaborate. No heart-tugging mission trips to orphanages in third world countries, just the fleeting thought of an awkward twelve-year-old prancing into gym class.

My younger brother Jay has Autism. Repeat my deep-rooted, intense love for another human being. I can't think of anything I wouldn't do for that dude. As we were growing up, I couldn't have predicted that he, too, would one day have artwork displayed in the Gift Garden. I never dreamed that I would later become an employee of the same organization, let alone that my future husband would one day be the CEO.

Naturally, I thought special education was the way to go, and proceeded to get a college degree. After applying to numerous schools, I never got a call. Not one. All I had ever known was beginning to feel foreign. I cried out to the Lord for the first time as relates to life's big issues. "Okay, God. I have this very expensive piece of paper here that is doing me ZERO good. Now what am I supposed to do?"

An answer to prayer came when my beloved former boss hired me at the County Board! Walking past the Gift Garden every day on the way to my office made my heart smile. My grandma would have been so proud. Bonus: I could see over the counter now.

Bryan was my co-worker long before he became my love. He, too, had spent the majority of his career working in the disabilities field. Bryan spent several years serving adults in residential group settings. In college, he majored in social work and had a heart for the underdog. I admired him. He answered my work questions. He kept to himself. He was a nice guy, a family man, and an excellent dad. Bryan remains a highly respected and well-loved leader within our disability community.

As we inched towards dating, I needed Bryan to be open to God's leading in regards to adoption. He chuckled and obliged, and a few years later we had a sweet little farm wedding in the same church where his parents and grandparents had exchanged vows. If there was anyone I wanted to travel the road of adoption with, it was this guy.

As we were settling into married life, we decided to slowly get the ball rolling toward adoption. We often talked about adoption with Bryan's two kids. Together, we looked at websites that featured babies and children who needed families. As best we could, we answered tough questions such as: "Where are their parents? Why is that big kid in a crib? Is that a boy or a girl? Why is he wearing so many layers of pink? How much is this one? How far away is that one? Why are there so many?" Those children on the websites all had two things in common: they all needed families and they all had special needs. We were already a family, and we happened to know quite a bit about special needs.

We desired permanency, so we chose adoption-only. Down syndrome was an easy choice, as God had been preparing our hearts for the special needs community our whole lives. Never did I develop a desire to carry a child in my own belly, but I always wanted a baby of my own to love. I caught wind of Bryan's baby-whispering skills and got to witness them myself. Private Down syndrome infant adoption is where we landed. My twelve-year-old gym class epiphany just got a bit more real!

We were reasonably familiar with the adoption process, since we knew several families that had adopted. Even so, we knew pursuing adoption of a child with Down syndrome would present some unique challenges, so we consulted with Stephanie at the NDSAN (National Down Syndrome Adoption Network).

Choosing Down syndrome adoption isn't only an emotional decision based on love; it needs to be heavily rooted in practical reality as well. Stephanie has pointed hundreds of families down the same path: find an adoption agency that is familiar with special needs adoption, get your home study completed, and then call her when it's done. Families cannot officially register with the NDSAN until their home study is complete.

Bryan refers to the NDSAN as "the broker" or "the middle man" in Down syndrome adoptions. They don't represent the birth family nor the adoptive family but work as a liaison to connect the two parties. Our home study adoption agency needed to understand and be agreeable with the fact that Stephanie would be linking us with the birth family. Our home study agency would step in again after the child was home for post-placement visits and finalization.

Choosing our adoption agency was not a challenge for us. We had colleagues employed there and trusted their experience with special needs adoption. After home visits, fingerprints, medical exams, a safety inspection, and more, it was time to complete the Characteristics Checklist. This intimidating form was an overwhelming reality check. We trusted the Lord would bring the perfect child to us, but we also needed to be honest with ourselves regarding which characteristics we were comfortable in handling and which we were not. Bryan was gracious in allowing me to check the box that indicated we would only consider girl referrals. We knew our list of what we could comfortably and confidently accept was short, but we trusted our big God to honor our sincerity.

Once our home study was completed, we focused our efforts

on fundraising to cover the costs. Although the NDSAN is completely free to both birth and adoptive families, both our home study agency and the birth parents' agency would have fees for their services. We quit dining out, skipped big vacations, and held local fundraisers. Asking friends and family for money to adopt a child is uncomfortable and awkward. We watched our online crowdfunding account grow almost daily and were humbled by others' generosity. A dear friend held a spaghetti dinner at our church, and nearly 400 people came. Folks we didn't even know showed up to cheer us on!

Unbeknownst to us, a friend—who happens to have Down syndrome—was in the process of raising $50,000 for various Down syndrome organizations in honor of his fiftieth birthday. One of his family members saw our journey on social media, and his whole family unanimously agreed to support our adoption. Game-changer! Almost overnight, we had all the funds we needed to take the next step: to officially register as a waiting family with the NDSAN.

As an official "waiting family," we now had to be prepared to bring a child home the very next day after our phone call came. We had readied the nursery. Suitcases were accessible. I dropped to part-time employment, with the ultimate goal of resignation. At the time, I was the founding director of the program for adults with special needs, so some strategy was involved in planning my succession. My employer (our church) and my boss were incredibly supportive: we went to work right away on posting my position. Since we didn't know when our adoption call would come, we collectively decided to terminate my employment on December 31. We had nine months to wrap things up and prepare the next director. The clock was ticking.

Birth parents looking to place their child for adoption come to the table desiring to see certain characteristics in the adoptive parents. Stephanie, at the NDSAN, queries the database of waiting families, which results in a list that fits the birth parents requirements. If a family comes up on the query, limited information is shared with them. The adoptive families are asked to consider the birth family's circumstance and let Stephanie know if they would like their profile shared with the birth family.

Two months into the waiting process, we got our first call. A boy. We were hoping for a girl. My work transition had just begun, and my successor had not yet been secured. The timing wasn't right, so we passed on this opportunity.

A few months later, a second call came; a baby girl, due in two months. A little sooner than ideal, but we could make it work. We threw our hat in the ring as one of six families to be considered.

After the initial queried list of six families, the birth family narrowed the group down to three that would be interviewed by phone. We were not chosen. Rejection is heartbreaking. We didn't know *why* we weren't selected, but we received a standard email from Stephanie explaining, in detail, that other families had been chosen to move forward. We would be placed back on the list of families ready for immediate placement.

December 31 was approaching fast. In late November, we received another call. This baby girl was due in early January and would be born in the state next to us. I would be completely finished with work and we wouldn't have to travel far; this was obviously what God had planned!

We were queried into round one and then chosen by the birth parents to be in the top three. But then a technicality materialized beyond our control. The birth parents' adoption agency would not consider any families in a remarriage situation where they had not yet been married for six years. We had only been married for three years at the time. We cried. We were mad. We begged the agency to bend the rules just this one time and let the birth parents make the call. Could we talk to their board? Could we find a loophole? This was our girl! But alas, the official email came from Stephanie. "Thank you for coming forward for this baby girl, but another family has been chosen. You have been placed back on the list."

Before, when we got these emails, I had cried. Cried a little for us, but mostly cried tears of joy that a baby had a family and a family had a baby. This time, the crying was for us; it was another round of heartbreak. This one hit us particularly hard. We had waited nine months so far. I was quitting my job, for goodness sakes, and still no baby. The nursery was dusty. I focused on finishing well at work, but my heavy heart was hurting.

On December 28, our nephew was born. At least someone in the family had a baby! As Bryan and I walked into the hospital to meet our new nephew, Stephanie's name appeared on my phone. We paused in the hospital lobby to jot down the details of this new situation. We weren't naive this time. We didn't get our hopes up. With shaky hands, I wrote, "Girl. Caucasian. High-risk pregnancy. Baby measuring small. Could deliver early." Wait, what? Two babies? Twins? I'd always wanted twins—this was not an issue at all! Wait, the sibling was not showing signs of Down syndrome. Only the smaller baby, the one with Down syndrome, would be placed for adoption. The birth parents would parent the typical sibling.

"Are you still interested?" Exhale. "Yes!"

We were back in the ring, one of six families again. We prayed for God's will to be done.

An unknown number from baby girl's birth state came late on a Sunday afternoon. It was a lady from the birth parents' adoption agency, calling to clarify a few items on our documents before presenting profiles later in the week. I wasn't sure why she couldn't wait until normal business hours, but I answered her questions anyway. It was a very technical phone call. I agreed to send all updated documents the next day.

Ten minutes later, there was a second call from the same number. I assumed she had forgotten to ask me something.

"Is your husband home? Can you go get him and put him on speakerphone, please?

"The birth parents have chosen you, she was born four days ago, and the birth parents are here on speaker phone right now."

Our eyes widened and welled up with tears; you could have heard a pin drop.

Such a mix of emotions all in one phone call: pure joy, fear, excitement, hope, and giddiness! My Fitbit recorded my heart rate at 110 beats per second. Twenty years after initially getting "the call" from God to adopt, we were now on a real call about a real baby who was really going to be ours. God's faithfulness is unparalleled!

All the while, on the other end of the call, we noted silence, tears, pain, sadness, grief, uncertainty, and exhaustion from her birth parents.

Adoption is born out of loss. There are two sides to every adoption story. Redeeming love is alone the work of Christ. We cling to His hope that is only born out of loss, a death to self, a relinquishing of rights, and the full release of control.

God taught me a new way to love right then and there on that phone call. I had instant and endless respect for our girl's birth parents, and still do. I have a love for them that I've never had for anyone else.

The phone call continued. Both babies were alive. It had been an emergency delivery on December 31, my last day of work. Our little girl was just over two pounds, and her birth report described her as vigorous, awake, and alert. She was small but stable. Both babies would remain side by side in the NICU for an undetermined length of time; weeks, maybe months.

The birth parents would visit both babies during the day and then return home each night. They asked that we wait until the weekend to travel to meet them and our girl, as they were drained and needed a few more days to get things in order. We were disappointed—we were ready to hop in the car that night, but respected their wishes.

The next two days were spent texting with birth mom and learning more about one another. She was an open book as relates to the pregnancy. She allowed me to ask questions, and responded with gracious answers. Things were going great, so we began telling close friends and family about our girl. It was difficult to contain our excitement! Birth mom sent pictures of the baby, and I noticed right away that she didn't have too many of the common physical characteristics of Down syndrome. Were they sure this baby actually had Down syndrome? More tests were being done to confirm.

We booked a hotel near the hospital for the weekend. Gifts were trickling in. On day three, the texting thinned. A call from the birth parents' adoption agency came that evening, informing us that the birth parents did not want us to travel yet, but were requesting that we delay our visit. They were putting the adoption on hold. It felt like a punch to the stomach. The rug was pulled out from underneath us. What was happening? We were falling in love with a baby that might not end up being ours.

Over the next few days, the birth mom continued to send pictures. My heart jumped. I thanked her and saved each one. It was bittersweet, as we had no idea what they were thinking or feeling, and we were cautious not to push the issue. We walked a fine line. They hadn't called the whole thing off, but there was no further talk of us coming to meet them, either. We learned about the term "failed adoption," and clung to Jesus. And waited. And waited.

Desperate for understanding, I offered to put on my case-worker hat and talk with birth mom on the phone, to answer any questions she might have. She agreed, and then said these words I'll never forget: "Maybe God gave me two babies so I could give one to someone else." What a thought! She had thoughtfully made her decision long ago and was ready to move forward with the plan. She wanted the absolute best life for her child, and she wasn't confident that she could provide it. She wanted her to have a stay-at-home mom, and she planned to continue working. She knew her baby girl would need therapies, and they knew their insurance wouldn't cover any. Birth dad was having a more difficult time with the decision. We all waited.

After nearly two excruciating weeks, we decided to buy a bigger vehicle. We hoped we'd need it sooner or later. As we were taking a test drive, I received another text from birth mom. "Are you still interested in adopting our girl?" Again, with shaky hands,

I responded with a resounding "ABSOLUTELY," and from the back seat, I let Bryan know that this time, we were officially getting our girl!

We met them in our hotel lobby. After nearly two hours of chatting, we must have passed their test, and followed them to the hospital. The NICU was full, so both babies had been moved to an overflow room. We remember every surreal detail. January 23, day twenty-four of her life. We looked at each other with tears welling up as we stood on opposite sides of her isolette and looked down at our teeny-tiny, two-pound ten-ounce girl. Her legs were the size of cheap hot dogs. My wedding ring fit perfectly in the palm of her hand. They asked if we wanted to hold her, and we could hardly believe it. Two hours ago we hadn't even known if we'd get to meet her; now we were changing her diaper and moving monitor cords around so we could hold her!

The birth parents were there, holding and tending to their baby. Peace surrounded us and joy was sewn into our hearts. We spent several more hours in that overflow NICU room. More than a few nurses moved into and out of the room, and I'm pretty sure they were just checking us out. Who were these people that came from out of state to adopt this baby with Down syndrome? And here they are, just hanging out with the birth parents in the same room, and everybody is smiling like this is normal! I have to admit that it was quite an interesting arrangement. But the Holy Spirit was present and guided our every move.

Birth mom took pictures of me holding our girl for the first time. I alerted the nurses that this baby was hungry, and they asked who wanted to feed our girl her first real bottle. Birth mom looked at me and told me it was go-time. Oh my goodness. How do you feed a two-pound baby a bottle that is half her size? She took to the bottle right away. Bryan was by my side, my constant cheerleader, as we passed her back and forth for hours.

We spent three more days in town, and then headed home to work on adoption paperwork. Our state requires home studies to be updated every two years. Their state requires paperwork to be updated annually, so we had some work to do. In forty-eight hours I had everything in motion and was headed back out of state. Bryan was back at work. We wanted to save his time off for when she came home for good.

For the next eight weeks, I took up residence with Bryan's aunt and uncle, who live only twenty minutes from the hospital. As empty nesters, they were thrilled to have guests and were especially looking forward to a baby coming to visit for a while. This saved us considerable housing and travel expenses. We were so grateful for their hospitality.

When it was time for more formal discussion, we met their adoption agency representative at the birth parents' home. They provided dinner, along with honest dialogue about our unique situation. We landed on a semi-open adoption. Visits would not occur, but us moms would keep in touch by texting and photo sharing. I plan to make a yearly photo scrapbook of our girl for both of us. Deciding how to handle this story with our girl's sibling was both delicate and tough. The further I wade into special needs adoption, the more I hear others' stories that aren't too far off from ours.

We didn't know what the future would hold for our little girl. Would she walk? Would she talk? What would her cognitive functioning look like? Would she understand the concept of adoption? How would her heart feel? Only time will tell, so we couldn't make any promises about what we would tell her about her birth parents. If she does understand someday, maybe we'll tell her that God gave her birth mom two babies, so she could keep one for herself and give us the greatest gift of all.

Our girl was always stable and healthy but remained in the NICU for a total of forty-seven days because she was just so small. Bryan would visit on weekends when his work schedule allowed and man, did we miss him when he was gone! When she was finally discharged, we had to use receiving blankets to prop her up in her car seat. She wasn't even four pounds yet! We returned to our home-away-from-home and stayed for another four weeks until we were officially permitted to leave the state and go home. We were finally all together again.

We were crazy about our girl even before she was ours. We missed out on twenty-four days of hugs and kisses, but we got to work right away making up for lost time. Our adoption journey was documented in our local newspaper. Friends held baby showers for us, and gifts were piled high and kept coming for months after we got home. Meals were delivered, and finding free babysitters has never once been an issue. I assure her birth mom often that this girl is overly loved and will never know any different.

Our capacity to love is bigger than we thought. Bryan's fear of not loving an adopted child as much as he loves his biological children was shattered. I knew when I saw all her little fingers wrapped around his pinky finger that one day it would be him that was wrapped around her little finger. We hope the big kids will someday recognize our obedience to God and will be proud to be a part of our family.

So, that's the way we became the Blended Bunch. Just a family after God's heart. Work, chores, and homework. Church, school, and therapies. Diapers and baseball games, braces and bonfires. Meals to be cooked, dishes to be done. We never said we'd stop at one…

…and we're still waiting for a live-in housekeeper/maid/cook to show up. So if our very own "Alice" is out there, come find us!

If you experience even the slightest heart tug toward adoption, it's not a mistake; it's a sweet, simple nudge. Sometimes God really does give a mother a baby to give to someone else.

This just in: Heckert Party of Six coming Summer 2019! Anna will be joining our family all the way from China! Born just 11 days before our girl, we'll finally have our Double Downs after all.

CHAPTER
SEVEN

His name is samuel

"I prayed for this child and God answered my prayer."
1 Samuel 1:27

He is a gift from God wrapped up in the cutest packaging. From the placement of a mole in the center of his neck to the space between his toes to his now round little belly (which was once quite thin) to his deep brown eyes, he is perfection. Filled with awe and wonder, love and joy, strength and resilience, curiosity and excitement, he lights up my life.

His easy ability to appreciate the beauty in the ordinary has caused me to now value what once I barely noticed, like the feel of raindrops, which he loves to catch on his tongue. Daily, he teaches us gratitude for what really matters. The small, often-overlooked moments such as taking walks, playing in puddles, and exercise classes are made special by his enthusiasm and joy in doing them. The things I once prioritized—such as cleaning and cooking—have moved down the list so that I can spend more time with him.

I could continue to brag on him and it wouldn't feel wrong, since I had no part in supplying his genes. You see, this little boy wasn't born into my family but rather chosen by us, through God, to be a part of our family. It has been a long and sometimes difficult journey, but one I am glad we have taken because I am now blessed to be his Mama from now until forever. I happily embrace this responsibility with all the love in my heart because this little boy has been our absolute best "Yes."

We are the Umstead family. My name is Heather, and I am a stay-at-home mama of four children. My husband, Tommy, is a wonderful man who is the foreman for a construction company. Our children are Derek, 25, Cody, 22, Sadie, 20, and Brady, 15. Derek and Cody now have homes of their own. Sadie lives at home and commutes to college, and Brady recently finished his freshman year of high school.

Tommy and I were close to that stage of life when our children were going to leave to make lives of their own. Although we were sad, we also embraced the idea that we would finally have our independence and time alone together. Since Tommy and I were married and had children at a young age, we looked forward to travel and dinners out, which weren't affordable with a large family. We also anticipated finally having the honeymoon we never experienced. We planned one for both our tenth and twentieth anniversaries, but it never happened, so we were determined not to allow our twenty-fifth anniversary to pass without a celebration. God, however, had other plans for us.

These plans didn't include the honeymoon, but we were to travel and go on an adventure that even Tommy and I couldn't have imagined. Our journey would take us to China, and it would give us the most wonderful addition to our already big brood. We would discover that the greatest happiness could be found in the unlikeliest of places and in the moments when God makes the plans.

I was fortunate that I was able to bear children with ease and that my children were born healthy. I, however, always had a desire to adopt and take care of a child with special needs. I often prayed to God about this feeling. "God," I prayed, "if you need a place for a special child, then I am your girl. I will welcome that child with love and joy." During the beautifully chaotic years of my children being small, I was often lost in the fast-paced world of motherhood, and my conversations with God turned to praying for the wisdom to keep my children safe and raise them well. Although my focus had shifted, my desire to take in a child never diminished.

Once my youngest son entered school, I started working with children in my school district who have autism. It was perfect! Not only was I able to work around my children's schedules, but I was also helping children with special needs. These students were a joy, and I believed this was what God had planned for me when He planted that small seed of desire in me to help a child in need. I was to learn, however, that it was only the seed.

In July of 2016, while on our way to the beach, I read a Facebook post from a friend, who was sharing it in hopes of finding a family for a little boy yet to be born. He was diagnosed with Down syndrome, and although his mother wanted to give him life, she felt unable to raise him. After reading it to my husband, I told him we should step up to raise him. He quickly and sternly replied, "No, Heather Elizabeth!" I knew that he, like my mother, meant business when he used my middle name, so I let it pass, deciding to keep it between Jesus and me.

While on vacation, I kept tabs on the Facebook post. I also researched the idea a bit more. First, I learned there are a whole lot of children who needed families! Second, I discovered that it isn't as easy as just "stepping up" to be the family. Still not discouraged by this information, I decided to revisit the conversation with my husband while sitting on the porch one evening. I now had the support of my son Cody, his fiancé Becca, and my daughter, Sadie, who all believed that adding a sibling was a great idea. Although Tommy rolled his eyes, this time he promised to think about it. We finished a great week at the beach with no more mention of adoption—at least not to Tommy.

After returning home, I thought about adoption daily. I researched and made phone calls, exploring all possibilities from domestic adoption to foreign adoption, from children with severe disabilities to children with only minor needs. It wasn't long before I had filled an entire notebook with information. In between my time researching, I prayed. What had begun as a desire now felt like a mission—one I wanted to do right. I wanted to hear God clearly because I knew this journey would have mountains that I could not climb alone. Knowing that God would already know the terrain, He was the one with whom I wanted to climb.

As much as I felt the desire to travel this path, Tommy didn't; he was my first "mountain." I refer to Tommy as my "mountain" not just because of his initial refusal to consider the path of adoption, but also because a mountain is a great representation of him. He is a strong and rugged man who stands bravely in the path of every storm, protecting and keeping his family safe. Tommy is a wonderful husband, a loving father, and a dedicated Marine whose service didn't stop with his country but extends to his family whom he faithfully guides through every valley. I knew that Tommy's role as our provider and protector caused him to be cautious about this "detour" in our lives; it posed a risk that he was, at this point, unwilling to take. I also knew, however, that I wouldn't be able to take this journey without him.

Adding a child to *us* meant that I didn't just need my husband's permission; I needed him to *want* this as well. I understood, though, that it was important for Tommy to not just succumb to my appeal, but to feel the seed that planted itself in my heart take root in his. For this to truly work, he needed not just to *allow* it; he needed to *want* it. So, I decided to pray until Tommy got on board, except he didn't.

One Sunday during the invitation at church, I went forward for prayer. I asked the man with whom I prayed to pray that either Tommy would share my desire or that God would remove it from me. I couldn't continue the way that I was, for it was consuming me. My desire for another child transformed from something positive to something negative that was weighing me down.

Three months passed. I thought Tommy had forgotten about my desire to adopt, but slowly he dipped his foot into the water, telling me that he would not travel outside of the United States. He also felt that the care necessary for a child with Down syndrome was more than he could consider. Happy with even the smallest inroads, I began to research the domestic adoption of children without a lifelong need.

God is specific in His calling, and the way I heard His words was deep within my heart. It was that gut feeling, an instinctive pull in a specific direction; His direction. My calling was **not** domestic, and it was **for** a child with Down syndrome. I tried so hard to fit my calling into Tommy's qualifications. I tried compromising my desire with my husband's wants. I researched domestically located children with Down syndrome and children with cleft lips who were located overseas. Nothing took root. What I was to learn—that God already knew—was that my child was waiting for me in an orphanage in Fuyang, China.

Tommy still wasn't fully committed to the idea when we saw Robert Jay (the name his agency gave him) on the Madison Adoption Agency's page. There he was, with one sock on and one sock off, and I knew. He was meant for me! Just as others predicted, I just "knew." Tommy agreed to pursue him. My first mountain was conquered.

The second mountain, however, soon loomed large in front of us. How would we find a way to pay the $40,000 necessary to adopt him? Although our family had everything we needed, we didn't have that amount in the bank. Our initial plans of taking a loan or borrowing from Tommy's retirement quickly fell short when we discovered that we could only withdraw the money for emergencies. Unfortunately, a child who would certainly die if not adopted didn't qualify as an emergency to the bank, even if it did to me.

We could have moved forward with a loan, but because we wanted to be debt-free as quickly as possible, we didn't feel comfortable taking out a loan. However, we also didn't feel comfortable giving up on Robert Jay.

We didn't want to ask others for help. We believed that God had placed this in *our* hearts, so we felt it was up to us to figure out what to do. We were discouraged. We now both felt this desire, this drive to adopt, yet we didn't see how we could manage it. So, I met with the local pastor's wife for coffee. She'd chosen the road of adoption, and I'd hoped she could guide me, which she did. She encouraged me to pursue fundraising. Tommy had already said "No" to that option, but I agreed. She proposed the idea with the intent of letting God "show up."

I wish I could say that I readily took her advice, but it took a while for me to come to it. Perhaps it was pride. In 2 Chronicles 7:14, it says, "If my people who are *called* by my name will *humble* themselves and pray…" I realized that we had to face the fact that our pride was not only threatening to keep us from what God was calling us to do but also keeping us from saving a life—the life of our "son." For the first time in our marriage, we prayed together as we started our second climb.

We decided to move forward with the fundraising. A good friend of mine suggested we host a Bingo night. Since she was experienced in fundraising, I trusted that this would be a good place for us to begin, especially since she said that Bingo would raise the most money. She speculated that 100 tickets sold would raise around $4,000. This was enough to get us started. So, I took money I'd secretly stashed away and reserved the fire hall and supplies. Our goal was to sell 100 tickets prior to Bingo day, which was March 4, 2017. Unfortunately, we'd only sold seven tickets two weeks prior to the event. I was starting to lose faith, worried that

I'd just sunk my personal savings into what would only amount to a fun day for a few of us.

What I couldn't have imagined was that we would have to turn people away from our Bingo. We had to stop selling tickets at the door because the social hall couldn't hold any more people. We had the largest 50/50 anyone had ever seen. People brought so many things for our Chinese auction that we ran out of tables. We also sold pizza, yet, although we had planned for only seventy-five people, we never ran out of food.

At the start of the day we'd hoped for $3,000 but, at the end of the day, we had raised almost $13,000! This win was confirmation that God could dream bigger than we could. I felt it was as though He was saying, "I've got this. You just keep walking." And so we did. One of the biggest messages I would love to share with others is that if you are considering adoption and God is calling you to it, then know He will get you through it.

On Monday morning we called to schedule our home study and also began the paperwork, which proved to be a monumental task. Next, we contacted the agency with Robert Jay's file. They told us they had lost his file on Friday, March 3. This news felt like a punch to the stomach. When an agency has a file for more than three months with no one showing any interest, the file goes back on the shared list, which I understood to be the Internet's black hole.

I made a request of four people in the adoption world to try and find him. I knew it was going to be difficult, since I didn't have his date of birth or his real Chinese name. It seemed as though what was once so certain was no longer clear at all. One night, after shedding a few tears, Tommy gently suggested, "Maybe he isn't our son. Maybe there is another family that would serve him better."

Bitterly, I snapped, "There is **no** better family that could serve him better than us!" I turned away from him and tried to fall asleep.

It was 11:10 pm and I felt neither asleep nor awake when I heard the text notification on my phone. I ignored it, thinking it was a wrong number. Again, I heard my phone. In my mind's eye, I saw the name of the beautiful lady who was advocating online for Robert Jay. I decided to get up and check. On my phone was a message from her, saying, "We found him!"

Although he had been found and was to be picked back up from the agency that had him, I had only three days to accomplish everything needed to secure his file, which meant that he was reserved for me only as long as I was deemed worthy of adopting him. I was worried I wouldn't be able to accomplish all the paperwork in such a short time but, again, God took care of me by sending a massive snowstorm. The schools closed for three days, providing me with the time I needed to write letters, get a doctor to review his file, and request to be his mom. On March 20, 2017 (our wedding anniversary), we received our preapproval from China; Robert Jay was being held for us. We were euphoric!

Euphoria wasn't the only emotion we felt or would feel during this adoption process. The entire experience was fraught with every emotion. We felt joy, sadness, excitement, defeat, dread, anticipation, and love. The rush of ever-changing feelings could be draining, and I often wondered if I would have the mental stamina to continue this journey.

My comfort to carry on came from my belief that God was guiding me. I prayed and carried Bible verses in my pocket. I placed verses under my pillow at night, and as I was falling asleep, I begged God to hold my hand while I traveled this road to its end.

His hand wrapped around mine is how I was able to take the next steps forward and bear not only my own self-doubt but also the doubt of those around me.

We live in a community where we are blessed to have people who support us. There were, however, those who questioned our choices on this path to adoption. Individuals who boldly, and at times harshly, asked, "Why China? Why don't you help an American child?" and, "You shouldn't do this if you can't afford it." The most heartbreaking of questions was, "Why would you ruin *your* life with a child who will need to be taken care of for the rest of *his* life?" Only words, but they left an imprint of doubt that caused me to question my own choice, but I moved forward. I believed that God's words would ring loudest in my ears if only I continued to listen.

We continued the fundraising with an online lottery, a tee-shirt sale, yard sales, a shoe drive, softball tournaments, a spaghetti dinner, a 5K, and a few other small activities. These efforts—along with a grant from Show Hope—met our goal of $35,000. We'd conquered our second mountain.

Our third mountain was by far the steepest, and one I never imagined would be a part of this journey. The height and breadth of this mountainous trial threatened to stop us in our tracks. It came not in the form of attacks from others but from an attack on my own mind. I began having symptoms of a heart attack. One was so severe that it sent me, panicked, to the emergency room. They diagnosed me with dehydration and sent me home.

The attacks didn't stop, though. My heart raced so significantly that I would be breathless. I was scared and I didn't feel in control of my thoughts, which ranged from a fear of dying to not wanting to be alone to questioning whether I was truly a child of God. After all, if I were God's child, why was He allowing this to happen to me?

My inability to care for myself also caused me to question if I could care for this precious life waiting for me in China. That fear spiraled into one in which I worried that if I were unable to carry out the adoption, others would view me as a failure and, possibly, a thief. I also felt the responsibility to other families who might want to adopt and needed to raise funds. What if my failure to follow through caused people not to help them? I was ashamed of myself for these feelings because I believed that I should be stronger, better, and wiser.

It soon felt like a fight I couldn't win, but after many trips to the doctor and lots of tests, I was diagnosed with a condition called SVT (Supraventricular tachycardia). It's when your heart beats very fast and out of rhythm. The doctors prescribed a medication that controlled my heart rhythm, but not my mind. I began to see a psychologist who explained to me that sometimes when one experiences so many emotions, it becomes like a combination lock that opens with the right numbers. *Pop!* My "safe" of anxiety and panic was opened wide.

Others had told me that the road to adoption is pitted with many bumps and potholes. I was ready to face their warnings of financial difficulties and logistical challenges, but I was not prepared to suffer an attack from within my own body. After four months of care, I was finally able to control what once seemed so out of control.

Having SVT was one of the most difficult challenges I faced, but upon reflection, it happened at the best time since it was during the period when all the important documents were signed and delivered, and we were just waiting. It was my greatest test, and I know now that God never left me; He simply challenged me. I believe He made me focus on the heart in my chest so that I could focus on the "heart" I needed for the rest of this journey. And, so, I climbed and conquered the third mountain.

In mid-November, we received word that we would travel to China to get our boy before Christmas. He would never spend another Christmas without a family. Alone when I got the news, I spun around and around in my living room as I praised God for getting us this far. By December 1, Tommy, Cody, and I boarded a plane to Beijing, China. I did better with the flight than I expected, even if the cramped space of the plane wore on me a bit.

We spent one night in Beijing and then boarded another plane in the morning for Hefei, the place we would call "home" for the first week and the place where we would finally set eyes on our son. The hotel was beautifully decorated for Christmas and created a sense of comfort for us. Hefei is a very traditional province where few people speak English, and so we were dependent on our guide and driver, Michael.

With no English TV channels and an apprehension to venture outside, we stayed in and window-watched, talked, and anticipated our first meeting with our son.

I slept the uneasy sleep of a child on Christmas Eve, excited with the anticipation of receiving my "gift."

The next morning we loaded the van and, with very little sleep and a lot of tears, drove to the government building where two other families also waited for their children to arrive. The money was exchanged and the paperwork checked.

I kept my eyes focused on the door as I waited for my Robert Jay to come through that very doorway. I, again, prayed the prayer

I'd recited daily; "Please let him know I'm his Momma." The door opened twice and each time my heart skipped, but each time it was for the other families. I watched as they hugged their new little girls. It seemed wonderful to me, but I remembered books warning that when children don't show the correct emotion, it can be because they don't have the ability to bond.

Again, another worry pressed against my mind, but it slowly dissolved as the door opened and this time my child, Robert Jay, or, Yang Shun Qian, was waiting in the doorway. Monday, December 4, exactly nine months from our beginnings. I couldn't help but think about how, just as four children had grown in my belly for nine months, Samuel had grown in my heart and mind for nine months.

I immediately knew it was him. The love in my heart overflowed, threatening to let loose the tears I withheld for fear of frightening him. Dressed in clothes much like a snowsuit, he could barely bend in half. A nanny held him, and I restrained myself from grabbing him from her arms. She pointed to me and said, "Momma." I knelt and took his little hands in both of mine and rubbed them gently. He turned away, scared. I kept rubbing his little hands, which were rough and dry. I begged him with my eyes to let me wrap him up in love and never let go. After a few minutes and a few tears, he allowed me to hold him. He continued to cry, not hard, but enough that we knew he was grieving. An angel who had been entrusted to so many, yet to no one, finally had a family, a home. He also, finally, had a name.

He would no longer carry the name given to all orphans, nor would he carry the name an agency gave to him. He would have the name his family deemed perfect for him. This little boy, so full of love and joy, strength and determination, this child of ours, is named "Samuel," a name that I found in a Bible verse that spoke to me. It's 1 Samuel 1:27: "I prayed for this child and God answered my prayer."

This was the prayer of Hannah after many years of being unable to have a child. Although being unable to bear my own children wasn't a plight I shared with Hannah, my desire to have a child that God deemed was meant for me was just as strong. And, so, his name is Samuel. It is a Hebrew name meaning, "God has heard," and He did hear. God not only heard my prayers as I sought to find and walk this path, but He also *heard* Samuel.

Because God heard and because I listened when God spoke to me, my family is now blessed with an amazing love for a child who brings us abundant joy, an even stronger sense of faith, and fills our days with an appreciation for each one. I know that many will say that we "saved" Samuel, but the truth that I know and God helped me to learn is that Samuel saved us.

CHAPTER
EIGHT

Kai's story

It was an early winter morning, and I could feel the chill outside of my warm down comforter willing me to stay in bed. I needed to get up and get my day started, but I just wanted to lie there and continue trying to process the dream that had just startled me awake. I stumbled into the bathroom to wash my face, hoping to become alert enough to determine what was real and what wasn't. As I recalled the vivid details of this dream, I had an overwhelming feeling that God had just shown me that we had a baby boy in China.

With his sweet face still fresh in my mind, I decided to wake up my husband, Brodie, and tell him about it. It was unusual for me to be up before him. But this dream had me up early on this particular morning, and I knew he wouldn't mind me waking him up to share. With four kids, our early morning talks had become sacred to us. Having time to pray and get on the same page each day was becoming more and more necessary as we were being called to balance more.

As I relayed the details of the dream to Brodie, he gently reminded me, "Babe, maybe we're just supposed to pray for that little guy? We don't even have Kaleb and Khloe home yet." He was right; how could I even think God would call us to adopt from China again in this season? We were in the final stages of adopting a sibling set from Haiti and were about to move there for the remainder of their adoption process, however long that might be. This was a big enough step of faith for our family of six. We had no idea how long we'd be there; we only knew that we felt the Lord nudging our hearts to go.

Brodie truly has the gift of wisdom, and his confidence in the Lord makes it easy to follow his lead. I agreed with him and resolved to go about my day, knowing there were enough hurdles ahead in just completing our Haitian adoption, let alone worry about whether God was calling us to adopt another child from China.

It was January, and we were finally back into our normal routine after all the holiday buzz. It felt good to be settling into our steady and predictable schedule. The crock-pot was filled with a roast and veggies for dinner; the smell of it filling our home comforted me that there would be one less thing to do later in the hustle-bustle of the afternoon.

Still, my heart was unsettled. That dream; I just couldn't shake it. It was as clear in my mind as when I was having it. Subconsciously, it had been running through my mind all morning. I kept seeing the dimly lit room that started off my dream. I could feel the pit in my stomach as I recalled not knowing where I was as I timidly walked over to the other side of the room. There I saw a

Chinese nanny holding in her arms the most precious baby boy I'd ever seen. He was all bundled up in a puffy green snow jacket, and all I could see were his beautiful, almond-shaped eyes and chubby, kissable cheeks. He looked to be about nine months old and in my dream, I instinctively knew I was his momma. This revelation filled me with complete joy, and I immediately reached for him and ached to have him in my arms. The nanny holding him waved her hand at me and firmly told me, "Not yet, not yet!"

That's when I woke up with a jolt and sat straight up in bed, almost out of breath. It was just a dream. But it felt so real, and deep within me, I felt as if I already knew this baby. And why did it keep replaying over and over in my head throughout the day?

Regardless, I knew Brodie was right. I concluded that praying for this little guy and his forever family over the next few months would be the best thing I could do for him. When spring came, we packed up our family, along with some basic necessities, and moved to Haiti with great anticipation of finally having our two newest babies in our arms and becoming a family of eight.

With all the unknowns of trying to navigate third-world living and helping our two newest family members adjust, I still prayed for the little guy from my dream, but not as often. After about four months, when we were just settling into this new and simple way of life, their paperwork was complete, and we made the journey back home. We settled back into life at home and thanked the Lord daily for adding these two to our family, praising Him that He makes the best families.

Just three short years earlier we had been a family of five with three biological kids and no thought whatsoever of adoption. Life was predictable and smooth, for the most part, and we planned to do our best to keep it that way. Thankfully, the Lord's plans prevail, and seemingly out of nowhere, He called us to adopt a little girl from China. Our eyes were opened as we saw orphans through God's eyes for the first time. Through her brokenness, He broke us in the most beautiful of ways.

During her first two years at home, we felt as if we were drowning in her past trauma; nevertheless, we knew if the Lord gave us another opportunity to love one of His little ones again, we'd say "Yes." Now here we were, a family of eight. All of us had been changed for eternity through adoption, and as we settled into our new forever, we couldn't help but stand in awe of the family into which Jesus had woven us.

School started, and our transition home was really quite smooth. The holidays came and went, and if I'm being honest, things had become so busy I rarely even prayed for that sweet boy from China anymore. However, around mid-winter, I had another dream. I'm really not a big dream person. In fact, I rarely remember my dreams at all. But I believe that Jesus desires to speak to each one of us, and sometimes He chooses to speak through dreams.

Being that this is a rare experience for me, after this second dream, I knew the Lord was trying to tell us something. Perhaps we really did have a son in China. I couldn't deny it anymore; He was at work in a way I couldn't yet understand. The exact same little boy was in this dream as well, only he looked about a year older. Right away that got my attention, as my first dream was almost exactly one year prior.

In this second dream, I instantly knew it was the same little guy, and I had the exact same feeling in my gut; this was our child. This time he was pressed against my chest, and I was holding him over my shoulder. I remember that he was wearing a diaper. I could feel it as I patted his little bottom, and he was *filled* with joy! He threw his head back, laughing, and I saw his face, that same sweet smile, those same captivating, almond-shaped eyes, only this time they were squinted almost shut because he was laughing so hard. And there was something distinct about his right eye. In my dream, I kept telling him to look at me with both of his eyes because his right eye seemed to wander a bit. "Look at momma," I kept encouraging him, until I realized he *was* looking at me. This stood out to me as I woke up and pondered this dream in my heart. I knew I needed to tell Brodie; clearly, the Lord was doing something. I knew it deep within me.

Again, Brodie was sure it was just a dream and that there was no way we'd be starting another adoption so soon after moving back home with Kaleb and Khloe. Although these dreams felt so real at the time, I had no other information to go on. So again, I resolved that I would pray even more fervently for this dream boy and that, if he was ours, God would reveal it to both of us at the proper time.

Just a few nights later I was laying our three youngest kiddos down for bed and felt this strong urge to check out our agency's "waiting children" list for China. Being that it was such a random thought, I assumed it was just my imagination, and continued with our bedtime reading. I reasoned that it had been years since I was on our agency's China waiting list, and I was certain the password had changed.

On and on I read to the kids, and stronger and stronger came this urge to check out that list. As soon as I had them asleep, I decided to follow this prompting and try to log on. I couldn't believe it; the password was the same! "Now what, Lord?" I felt His soft whisper in my heart; "Just look and tell me what you see." Of course, I saw dozens of faces of precious, vulnerable children who didn't choose to be abandoned, who didn't choose their special need; children who were waiting for someone to want them, desperate for a brave and willing family that would love them as Jesus loves.

Down, down, down the list I scrolled, until there was a face that literally took my breath away. It was him! The baby's face from my first dream, identical, down to the snow jacket! How could this be? What was happening? Deep in my gut, I knew this was our son. I clicked on his sweet face to see his age and what his special need was. He was two-and-a-half years old, and his need was Down syndrome! "What? Lord, there's no way! We are so unqualified for that! We know nothing about Down syndrome, plus we just got home months ago and are in the thick of bonding with our two newest kiddos, and we still feel totally in over our heads most days with six, let alone seven, kids, and one with Down syndrome! Jesus, You know we can't handle that!"

His response seemed as if it was already settled deep in my spirit. "You're right, you can't handle a child with Down syndrome. You can't even handle what I've already entrusted to you. It is *I* who works in you to work according to My good purposes. Apart from Me, you can do nothing. But with Me, all things are possible!" An all-encompassing peace came over me, and I knew in that sacred moment that He was indeed asking us to love this child and be his forever family. He wasn't just asking us; He was *inviting* us to love this child as He loves him. He perfectly knit him in his birth mother's womb for a miraculous purpose. He was made for God's glory! I was infused with confidence from His Spirit and knew without a doubt that He would move mountains to bring this child home.

I couldn't wait to tell Brodie. It's one of the things I love most about our closeness; neither of us can wait to share everything with the other. Still, part of me was hesitant. I knew the special need of Down syndrome would overwhelm him, as it did me. But I was so confident in what the Lord was doing I went to tell him right away. Certain that his heart would be stirred in the same way mine was, I asked him if we could sneak back into our room, away from the big kids, so that we could talk privately.

I shared what had just happened and how I had seen this sweet baby's face from my dream and how I knew without a shadow of a doubt that God was indeed showing us our son. He was shocked, but we trust one another deeply, and he knows my heart is just to do whatever the Lord wants for us. Despite all this, he said his answer was a firm "No." He believed that my dreams meant something, especially now with seeing this child's face, but he just couldn't imagine that God would be asking us to adopt again, let alone a child with such significant needs. He felt confident that these dreams were for some other purpose and must have some other meaning. I was devastated.

How could the Lord be so clear with me and not align our hearts? After all, as husband and wife, we are called to be one in the Lord. I asked God *why* I was feeling this child was ours when Brodie was adamantly sure he wasn't. I felt in my heart as if God said, "I can change his firm 'No' to a confident 'Yes' in a moment; just trust Me."

With both of our other adoptions, the Lord lead Brodie's heart first; it was so much easier for me to follow his lead and just trust that Jesus was guiding us. Now it was me who heard the Lord first, and I found myself doubting everything I felt He was speaking to my heart. One thing we both knew for sure was that the Lord was doing something beyond our imaginations. We just needed to press in deeper to find out what that was.

I asked Brodie if we could request this little boy's file to find out more about him. For all we knew, there would be another significant need that he had which would make it clear that we couldn't handle his needs at this time, and we could move forward with just praying for him. Brodie thought this was a great next step, so we contacted our agency the following morning. They were thrilled to send us his file. It had been with them for a while, and they were only weeks away from sending it back to the massive China "shared list" where they wouldn't be able to advocate for him anymore. They sent the file right away with every bit of information they knew about him.

I eagerly opened the file and was elated to see it also had updated pictures. Of course, I jumped straight to opening the pictures. I couldn't believe the first picture that came through. The *exact* little face I saw in my second dream where his right eye drooped a little! As I looked at his gentle, joyful face, I felt deep in my spirit that I already knew this child! In all three of our other adoptions, I had never had this feeling. He was ours, and I knew it! Now Brodie really knew the Lord was doing something beyond what our human minds could wrap around.

We decided to take some time and really pray and seek God's clarity and beg Him to align our hearts. We took three weeks and did a twenty-one-day Daniel's fast (Daniel 10:2, 3). This makes us sound super spiritual but, really, we are just super desperate to get right this one life to which Jesus has called us. We always say we will do anything He asks, until the *ask* comes and the reality of what we are being asked to do hits us.

The truth is, following Jesus is sometimes hard. It was never promised to be easy. He even told us that in this world we *will* have trouble (John 16:33). But He assures us that we can be encouraged, even in hardships and difficulties, because He has overcome the world and therefore that means He has already overcome everything we will ever face or walk through! Convinced by these truths, we entered those three weeks with great expectancy. The Lord knew our hearts. He knew that our spirits were willing but our flesh was weak. We knew He honored our desire to get it right, even if we didn't know exactly what the right thing was in that situation.

In the last week of our time of fasting and praying, Brodie and our oldest daughter, Kennady, headed back to Haiti for a friend's wedding. Living there, we had made some really sweet friendships, and Kennady was asked to be a bridesmaid. With all the wedding activities Kennady was juggling each day, Brodie had a lot of time alone, just he and Jesus. As he pulled away from the busyness of life and had time to hear the Lord's Spirit testifying with his spirit, it became very evident to him that the Lord was, in fact, asking us to walk with Him into the unknown of adopting a child with Down syndrome. I, too, continued to feel this revelation with more and more confidence as I prayed during those few weeks.

I so respect how Brodie processed all of this. He trusted and knew that Jesus was revealing something through those two dreams. As he continued to seek God's will, he knew what God was asking us to do. But, as he says, he needed to grieve. He needed to grieve what *his* plans and dreams for our lives and our future were. We have no idea what our future will look like, but what we do know is that it will be very different now. I admire how he processed and even mourned giving up his dreams and desires for our future. As he says, we don't have to be *excited* right away about what God calls us to do, we just have to move forward in faith and trust that He will work it all out.

With our hearts aligned and confident that we were following the Lord's will, we began the necessary paperwork. Thankfully, as we waited, we connected with many wonderful families who had children with Down syndrome. These contacts were such a blessing for us. We went from fearfully obeying to actually being excited about this sacred journey of Down syndrome on which the Lord was inviting us. It seemed like all of a sudden, everywhere we went, we met both children and adults with Down syndrome. Our whole family would get so excited each time we met someone new with an extra chromosome. We were just beginning to enter this new and wonderful world, and we soon realized we had been missing out all these years by not knowing anyone with Down syndrome.

The China adoption process was seamless and quick. Before we knew it, we were flying across the ocean to get our precious boy. I can't explain it, but every part of me felt like I already knew him. Those dreams had been so real, and I couldn't wait to have him in my arms forever. We enjoyed sightseeing the day we arrived, and tried to keep ourselves awake to fight off the tidal wave of jet lag. Our uncontrollable exhaustion finally overtook us, and we collapsed into bed around seven that evening.

After a full night's sleep, we began to feel life ease back into our bodies as we rose before the sun. We eagerly got ready and went down to breakfast, hoping to get to our boy as soon as possible. Hardly able to wait another minute, we got onto the bus with our travel group and headed to the civil affairs office. We walked straight in and there he was, sitting on the couch, just chilling and taking in all the sights. We immediately got down on his level and handed him a toy that lights up when you touch it. He smiled, that same smile I already knew so well, deep in my soul. We offered him snacks, and he happily took them. Soon our initial paperwork was done, and it was time to head to the store and then back to our hotel room to settle in for our first night with our cherished new arrival.

I strapped him into the baby carrier and off we went. He never looked back. He snuggled right into me in that carrier, as if he'd been pressed against my chest a thousand times. Back at the hotel, he enjoyed giving each of us a turn holding him and even comfortably cuddled in our laps for long periods of time. I couldn't help but wonder if, in his heart, he felt as if he knew us, too.

Later that evening he developed a fever, which just kept spiking higher and higher. I thought maybe it was from all the stress, but by the next morning, I could tell he felt miserable. Still, he remained easy-going and even tried to give us a few smiles here and there. But it soon became evident we needed to have him checked, so our guide took us back to his orphanage to be seen at their hospital.

This was the most amazing orphanage I'd ever seen. It had a full hospital and school on campus. The staff was courteous and took great care of our little Kai. We found out, after blood-work, that he had scarlet fever and would need IV antibiotics for the next few days. He was a champ and lay there for hours each day in my arms as the IV ran through a vein in his forehead. It broke my heart to see him in so much pain, but I treasured the hours of bonding and meaningful eye contact. More than anything, I thanked Jesus that for the first time in little Kai's life, he had a family to wrap around him and do whatever it took to comfort him. Within a few days, he was recovering and back to his playful self. We were now headed to the grand province of Guangzhou for our final stretch of paperwork.

Kai's transition was so smooth and beautiful. We kept waiting for him to freak out or grieve, but he just kept loving us more and more each day. We enjoyed having those few weeks in China to bond and begin attaching, but we were so ready to get home to the rest of our family. Feeling a sense of awe and adoration, we thanked the Lord for entrusting us with this child. We boarded the plane late on our last night there and slept most of the way home. Little Kai never made a peep. He just gave sweet smiles and high-fives to curious passengers as they watched him in wonder.

Thankful to be home, we stayed up late that night, letting our kids who didn't travel with us soak in some precious sibling time with their new brother. It was as if he had been with us all along. Not wanting the sacredness of the evening to end, we forced ourselves to go to sleep and slept peacefully, enjoying the comfort of our own beds. Even Kai seemed to know that he was home. We woke up for the first morning as a family of nine and were so thankful for the Lord, once again, stretching us out of our comfort zones with His good and perfect ways.

We went into this adoption feeling as though we were making some sort of sacrifice for God. Like, "Okay Lord, we know there's this child who needs a family, and we know You want to love him through us, so even though we're worn out and tired, we will do this for You." But as soon as Kai was in our arms, we realized we weren't being asked to sacrifice at all. We were being given an extremely rare and precious gift, the gift of a child with an extra chromosome who loves at a level we had never experienced before. A child who quickly forgives and makes us want to do the same for one another. A child who helps us slow down and enjoy the simple things, like bubbles in the sink and walks around the yard, exploring bugs and piles of dirt as if for the first time every day.

Everything turns into a game with Kai, and sometimes he belly laughs so hard I have to lift him up to help him catch his breath. We would never have imagined how his loyal and constant love would teach us more about Jesus' love than anything else we've ever experienced. All of our fears quickly diminished, and we all fell head-over-heels in love with him.

Life at home as a family of nine is beautiful and lively; peaceful, yet full. Full of the beautiful and hard work it takes to transition a new child home, full of diapers that we swore we'd never have to change again, and full of laughter so deep our sides ache at the end of each day. It's days full of teaching and re-teaching, role-playing and re-do's, hours filled with doctors appointments and learning about all the complications that can come with having an extra chromosome. But full, mostly, of siblings growing into best friends and the fatherless learning a family's love that will never end. Jesus says, "I have come that they may have life and have it in all its fullness" (John 10:10).

More than anything, adoption—and Down syndrome adoption, specifically—has taught our family about the fullness of life found when we follow the call of our Lord, no matter what that call may be. Sometimes the step of faith feels too great, like we surely couldn't handle what He is asking. And the truth is, just like I felt His Spirit remind me as we were praying through our decision to adopt Kai, we can't handle loving and caring for a child with needs that are beyond our capacity to understand. But *He* can. And with Him, we can do all things.

CHAPTER
NINE

sam's story:
when the road darkens

Faithless is he that says "farewell" when the road darkens.

This timely quote from J.R.R. Tolkien's classic trilogy, *The Lord of the Rings,* was my mantra during one of the most tumultuous seasons of my life.

In the spring of 2013, our family was finally approved by our state to adopt a child with Down syndrome, a dream that had been growing in our hearts for a while. Three months later, during that long hot summer, we received a phone call that appeared to be the start of a new adventure. A wee one had been born, and his birth family felt unable to provide ongoing care for his different needs. I was pregnant with hope, thrilled by this potential match.

Thirty-six hours later, we learned that this boy would not be ours to raise. New to the feelings of rejection that often accompany the adoption road, we were devastated. Between heaving sobs and tight hugs, our two children cried out that muggy

August evening, "We'll never get a baby!" Despite my efforts to console them, I silently wondered if they might be right.

Since our days of dating, my husband and I had considered adoption as an option for growing our family someday. As a kid raised in an adoptive family, I was aware of the challenges—but also the deep joy—that comes with adoption.

In the late summer of 2012, we had reached a point in parenting where the kids required less hands-on care. They played well together (with the occasional squabble), were potty-trained, ate independently, and understood their boundaries within our home and beyond. In this new season, we began to wonder, "Are we being selfish by choosing to be 'done' with kids? What is our response to the many children who need a loving home? Are we willing to expand our family? What would that look like? Who are the most vulnerable children? Do we only exist to raise 'good' kids, send them on their way, and 'take it easy' until we die?"

Those questions led us to books, articles, and websites all pointing to the sobering fact that kids with disabilities are more likely to be abused and pushed to the streets—and least likely to be adopted—once they age out of their country's foster care system.

Our hearts shattered as we read the stories and discovered the dark truth that so many kids around the world are abandoned, discarded, and left to die because of their disability.

A few months after our research and secret conversations began, our daughter told us of a dream she had. When asked to share specifics, she said, "I dreamed that you and Daddy went to the brown house and picked out four babies." She even had each baby named. Then our precocious five-year-old asked a question that still haunts me; "Mommy, who will take those babies if we don't?"

At the time of her dream, we had not said a word to anyone about the possibility of adoption, although we had been talking behind closed doors for a while. The timing of our more recent prayers and conversations wove in so beautifully with our daughter's dream that we decided to pursue adoption with more intention.

As we bid farewell to 2012 and embarked on a new year, we set out on the road of adoption. Our desire was to provide a home for a wee one with an extra chromosome. In all of our reading and study, we learned that many women choose to terminate their pregnancy when they discover that the child they carry has Down syndrome. Their decision may be due to misinformation from doctors and geneticists, who often paint a very dark picture for these families.

In their efforts to educate, medical professionals may provide a rather limited perspective on Down syndrome. They fail to share or simply do not know the stories of beauty that can bloom in the midst of an unexpected, overwhelming diagnosis. We wanted to help provide an alternative for a birth family in a difficult situation and to provide a home for a child in need of a family.

We soon found ourselves navigating the complex, often demanding world of adoption paperwork. After choosing an agency, taking the appropriate legal steps, and paying the required funds, we were eventually home study approved. We registered with the NDSAN (National Down Syndrome Adoption Network, a matching agency specifically for children with Down syndrome), continued to apply for grants, and devoured every book available on adoption and Down syndrome.

As we began to share about our new adventure publicly, many friends and family members were supportive; however, we also faced questions that left me stunned, unable to respond intelligibly:

"You have the perfect family—why would you adopt a kid with a disability?"

"You have one girl and one boy—the million dollar family. What more could you want?"

"You have two beautiful, healthy children. Why would you do this to them?"

"You know this is forever, right? Like, you'll never really be done parenting?"

While I suspect these questions were meant to help us process the magnitude of our decision, I also wondered why some people felt the need to question our logic, our motives, and even our sanity. At times I felt as though I had to assure the naysayers that we were indeed thinking clearly and praying fervently. Despite the doubts of others, we were convinced in our hearts that this was the road we were to travel—the one that God had led us on—no matter the potential obstacles, unexpected turns, or future outcomes.

With the exception of that first phone call, the summer of 2013 was quiet. All we heard during those few months were the sweet prayers of our children; "Dear God, please bring our baby brother or sister home real, real soon."

In December of 2013, we received a phone call about a possible match. Within twenty-four hours, we learned that we were not chosen. Weeks later, we received a phone call about a potential international-to-domestic adoption case and waited for two weeks, only to learn that this case would remain strictly international. At the end of the month, we received a phone call about another birth family. Surely, we thought, this would be "the one."

We spent most of January sharing details of our lives with a prospective birth family, which we eventually met. After we drove away from our time with them, my weary, throbbing head dropped in my hands as I cried out to my husband, "They're not going to pick us! They're not going to pick us!" After an emotionally draining day, I came home and went on a cleaning spree. While on my hands and knees furiously scrubbing black scuff marks off an old linoleum floor, hot tears fell, leaving dark spots on my worn jeans. As I stopped to catch my breath, a deep sense of peace washed over me as I knew that this baby was not meant to be ours.

My suspicions were confirmed a few days later when we learned that we were not the intended choice. The shadows on this difficult road were growing. These denials were hard to accept without taking them personally. I often wondered, "What's wrong with us? What are we lacking? Are we pathetic, desperate losers? What about our family is so unappealing?"

I began to doubt my emotional resolve to continue. As I wrestled with my insecurities in the midst of the unknowns, I slowly began to see that each devastating "No" had less to do with others' perceptions of me and more to do with whether I would remain faithful when the adoption maps were shredded, the GPS silent, and the topography marked with dark valleys.

In March of 2014, we received two phone calls about two potential matches. But neither case brought a child to our home. I began to think that maybe I wasn't fit for the challenges of this road. I was no longer asking whether we *would* leave this adoption road but whether we *should*. Maybe the proverbial dead ends were actually meant to redirect us. Perhaps they were warning signs to leave the road before we encountered further heartache. Should we endure no matter how dark the road? No matter the financial obstacles or feelings of insecurity? Could we still be at peace along the way despite the overwhelming shadows that seemed to stalk us?

As those concerns plagued me, I was reminded of our purpose: To parent a child with Down syndrome, to bring hope to a birth family, and to advocate for this beautiful population. Maybe the darkness was meant to strengthen my endurance and courage, to push me to deeper places of trust in the One who had led us this far.

In April of 2014, we received a phone call about another potential baby. Within a week, we learned that the birth family had chosen another adoptive family. Although we were disappointed, we were less surprised this time and filled with more resolve than ever. My perspective had begun to shift. Perhaps my feet, worn from the miles, were growing calloused, roughened, and ready for the next step. The darkness along the way seemed to be doing the good and necessary work of building my endurance and courage. During this month, we updated our home study and continued to move forward, knowing that each day brought us closer to our little one.

Then came the unforgettable month of May. While sitting at my desk, updating our adoption profile, I got the overwhelming sense that Stephanie, our contact for the NDSAN, was going to call about "our" baby. Brimming with confidence and a hope beyond the valleys, I stood up from the desk and walked toward the phone, which had yet to ring. Ten steps later, I heard that pleasant, familiar chime echo from the kitchen. The caller ID revealed: STEPHANIE NDSAN. She shared of a baby boy due in August. I stifled a sob. I knew this baby was meant to be ours. The shadows along the road had slowly begun to fade.

The next two months allowed time for us to contact the birth family and wind our way through the complex legal matters for out-of-state adoptions. We made tentative travel plans and continued to pray for the family as they prepared for his birth and their difficult decision.

In August of 2014, we left home to meet with our son's birth mom at a local picnic area. As we got out of the car and released our kids to run, a tired woman slowly, tentatively approached me. Her swollen belly pressed against me as we greeted each other with broad smiles and a strong hug. I was so grateful for this sacred time to hear her story—to learn the details of her decision to choose another couple to parent the son she so deeply loved. She relinquished her right to parent, believing he needed more than she could provide. This was sacrificial love. This was brave love.

The next day we connected with the birth family at the hospital, assuring them of our love and support. As labor pains increased, we left the hospital to eat dinner and savor that quiet time as a couple. An hour later, just as we paid our bill, our cell phone rang. In a happy, relaxed tone, the doctor announced, "Hello, Mrs. Carper! Your son is here. He looks great! You can come meet him now in the NICU."

My son. *My son.* I bowed my head and wept with joy.

We returned to the hospital to be with his birth family before going to the NICU to meet him. As I walked into their room, the nurses and aides never made eye contact with me. Despite being invited into this space by both the doctor and the birth parents, I awkwardly shuffled away from the bed to the opposite wall, where I was welcomed by our son's birth father, a kind and gentle soul, quick to smile even amid his own loss. Thick, black braids framed his dark face, now glistening with tears. We embraced and thanked each other profusely.

By then, the nursing staff had moved away from the birth mother's bed, and I met her eyes. Deep hazel pools of both sadness and relief, puffy from exhaustion, tired from the act of giving birth, of giving over the one she so bravely carried for nine months. Trying desperately to conceal my emotions, to appear stronger than I felt, I moved my hand to my mouth to hide my quivering lips. I was afraid of the tears, afraid they wouldn't stop if they began to fall, afraid to appear weak and incapable of caring for this child to whom I'd been entrusted. She saw my struggle and quietly, almost timidly, asked, "Are you okay?" I could no longer maintain the façade of strength that I had tried so hard to build. I answered through quiet sobs, "It's bittersweet. Our great joy has come through your great loss. It's just bittersweet." We held each other, unashamed of our tears, welcoming both the joy and the pain of this journey. Two desperate mothers clinging tightly, two weary travelers on two very different roads, but somehow joined in our dreams for this wee one now present in the world.

An hour later, the hospital's social worker led us to the NICU. We chatted quietly with this kind, reserved woman in a white lab coat. Speaking in a no-nonsense tone, she curtly answered my questions and just when I thought this hospital needed a course in "How To Extend Hospitality to Adoptive Families," she said, "This is the first adoption I've known to be friendly. Most are full of fighting and drama." Before I could respond, she swiped her nametag and took us to another area beyond a large set of grey metal doors. She abruptly switched topics and began instructing us on how to wash our trembling hands with iodine soap. She introduced us to our son's NICU nurse, passed the proverbial baton, and then she was gone.

The kind and reassuring nurse led us down the short NICU hallway, past a new dad holding his tiny bundle, and new parents snuggling their fresh-from-God twins. We turned a corner and then I saw him. He was not swaddled or snuggled or held. "Baby Boy -------" was printed on his tag.

I stood over the clear plastic bin that held our newborn babe and through blurry eyes, marveled at his features. His hair was jet black and straight. His almond-shaped eyes were closed as if he dreamed of a world beyond these pale yellow walls. His adorable button nose had a clear tube running down to a machine that beeped intermittently. A yellow tube snaked from his tiny mouth to another machine beyond his plastic crib. His hands were outstretched as if asking me for a hug. His white Pampers deepened the tone of his mocha-colored skin. His tiny, wrinkled feet extended to the edge of the bin.

"His name is Samuel Creed Carper," I told the nurse. "We'll call him Sam."

I wondered if he knew how deeply I loved him. Did he feel the loss that brought him to us? Did he know the pain his first mama suffered down the hall? Did he sense the guilt his second mama carried? Did he know how fervently we had all prayed for him? Did he know that his life was a gift to us? To this world? I breathed a shaky, tearful prayer of thanks to the One who had led us to this place full of wonder and grief and beauty.

That evening, Sam was driven to another hospital with a more sophisticated NICU, where he had surgery to correct an abdominal issue. The highly trained transport team arrived in their green jumpsuits and began the tedious process of disconnecting all the wires and tubes and reconnecting them to their portable machines.

The transport team driver—a tall, older gentleman with a voice like James Earl Jones—leaned over to me, shook my hand, and said, "Congratulations, Mom. He's adorable."

Nearly a month later, with medical and legal issues resolved, we returned home to settle into real life as a family of five.

In our efforts to recall the details of our adoption journey, we realized that Sam's birthday was also the birthday of the baby we learned of that hot summer evening—our first rejection that left us bereft and bewildered. Exactly one year later from that first "No," we were given our "Yes."

Sam is now an active preschooler, full of mischief and joy, reaching milestones at his own pace, and well-loved by so many.

At times, this adventure, full of uncertainty and risk, made it nearly impossible for us to believe that the darkness would give way to light. The continual dead ends, the unpredictable wait time, and the medical uncertainties were all good reasons to change course. Choosing to leave the road of adoption would have been the safer, more predictable choice for us, and one that I would never judge another for choosing.

Being faithful to the journey and staying open to the lessons and risks along the way was the choice we knew we needed to make for our family. We were meant to connect with a specific birth family and a specific baby born at a specific time. If we had bid farewell when the road darkened, we would have missed the joyous light found in one remarkable baby boy.

CHAPTER
TEN

aDeLine's story

As I have been thinking about our family's adoption story, I want to share that, at the core, it's all about our relationship with our loving God. He showed up in the midst of the beautiful chaos that is our life and invited us to join Him on a mission to bring an orphaned child into a home where they will be loved and cherished. I am thankful His nature is patient because I can be slow to surrender sometimes; He has, however, led us on a remarkable journey of trust and obedience.

This is our story. Our testimony to His realness and faithfulness, even when I wanted to give up and potentially miss out on this beautiful blessing that is adopting a child with Down syndrome.

To start with, we are just an average, ordinary family. Maybe a bit larger than some and, then again, smaller than others. There are eight of us in all. My husband, Jeff, myself, Christy, and our tribe, from oldest to youngest: Jonah, Ella Grace, Haylee Joy, Caroline Faith, Judah, and our newest addition, Adeline Hope. The beginning of what we are today started almost twenty-two years ago on a dusty balcony in Port-au-Prince, Haiti.

I was nineteen and on my first of many trips abroad to the most impoverished country in the western hemisphere. I had been dreaming of experiencing foreign missions since my first-grade teacher, who was also a missionary, initially introduced me to Jesus. She taught me about how His Holy Spirit lives in His children; helping them, guiding them, and sometimes leading them on amazing adventures all around the world.

My turn had finally come in June of 1996, and I found myself in another world. The culture shock took me by surprise as I stepped out of the airport and into the hot Haitian sun. A sea of shouting people surrounded me; horns honked, dust billowed, and oh, the children. Unattended kids were wandering around half-clothed, and most of them barefoot. I was overcome with emotion. The guilt of having so much and taking it all for granted hit me hard, turning my stomach.

So, of course, as any person who has never experienced culture shock before might do, I began to hand out everything in my carry-on to the children who were outside the airport gates. Starting as a small group of two or three young kids, this quickly became a mob of grabbing, desperate arms yelling, "Miss Blanc, give me, give me! Miss, Miss…" I gave away every fruit snack, peanut butter cracker, and piece of candy I had as I was shoved into a steaming hot oven of a car by some of our leaders. Unable to breathe, we rolled down the windows to be greeted by arms reaching in, hoping for a prize in return.

I had never seen such need before in my life. The following morning was a Sunday, and we were able to attend a local church service, where the freedom and love of Christ were overwhelming in a completely different way. Although the level of poverty was staggering, the abounding joy that overflowed from their hearts to give all they had, whether it be their worship or their material things, was a stark contrast to some of the churches I had attended in the States. They were rich in ways that I wasn't. It was all I could do to hold back the tears on both accounts.

Sunday evening, I sat alone. I'm an introvert by nature, and sometimes I need to step away from the crowd to reflect and recharge. I sat on a bench scribbling my heart out into my brand-new "first mission trip" journal, when I heard a friendly, light-hearted voice greeting people coming up the stairs. As he came around the corner, I looked up to meet the kindest, darkest brown eyes I'd ever seen. The outgoing, people-person type, he introduced himself to me and laughed about the fact that "Weren't you the one who three weeks ago didn't even have a passport?" Yes, that was me, and it was indeed a miracle that it arrived in time to go on this trip. Well, as it turns out, this sweet, brown-eyed guy had a guitar and I had a songbook, and as we like to say, the rest is history! A divine appointment on the balcony of Wall's Guest House in Port-au-Prince brought us together.

This trip and time in my life were monumental. Not only did God introduce me to my future husband, but He was also drawing me closer to Himself. Up until that point, I tried hard to please God by following the rules and making, for the most part, good choices. As a self-critical perfectionist, I still knew I fell short of God's standard. But, to be honest, I was going through the Christian motions in my own strength. I was miserable and exhausted, trying to live this unattainable righteous life for Christ.

But, in the spring of 1998, during a challenging time of transition in my life, Jesus called me to completely surrender my all to Him. His word from Zechariah 4:6 (NIV) that says, " 'Not by might nor by power, but my Spirit,' says the Lord Almighty," brought peace to the growing anxiety in my heart. He knew I was weary and He promised that if I just came to Him, He would give me rest for my soul. And He did! Such an enormous weight was lifted off my shoulders, and at the same time, a whole new outlook for my life came into view.

Jeff and I married on December 19, 1998. We made the decision early on in our marriage that first of all, as God is our helper, we would always seek to honor Him and, secondly, that we would never speak of divorce; it was not an option. Now, anyone who has been married for any length of time knows it's tough work, and we learned the hard way, as most couples do.

This quiet introvert is quite the leader in heated yelling matches, and my sweet, extroverted, people-person husband can shut down, quiet as a mouse. It's honestly by God's grace alone that we are here today and still committed to each other. Our selfishness and stubborn pride could have torn us apart, but thankfully, we believe God's Word, that He who began a good work in us will faithfully complete it. The hard times have grown us and deepened our love and respect for each other. We can testify that marriage can work if you choose to commit to each other, in good times and bad, rich or poor, as long as you both shall live.

Then, the kids began to arrive! Not long after September 11, 2001, we found out we were expecting our first child. Such a fearful time and here we were, starting our family in a world that seemed more dangerous than ever. It brought us to our knees, and we began to pray God would bless us with children who would place their faith in Him and who would grow to be mighty leaders of their generation for Christ.

On May 27, 2002, our firstborn, Jonah, arrived, and we were simultaneously smitten with his precious dimpled face and overwhelmed in our new role as parents. Two of our beautiful daughters came next, Ella Grace on October 22, 2004, and Haylee Joy on March 26, 2008. Then we lost a baby. It was three months after Haylee was born that I found out I was pregnant with baby number four. It came as quite a shock, and I had great fears that this child wouldn't be a healthy baby. At our twelve-week ultrasound, the baby's heartbeat couldn't be found, and a day later, a D&C was scheduled.

I did not recover well from this and suffered through depression and anxiety for about a year. In all the pain, Jeff stuck to me like glue. His unconditional love for me through my lowest moments pointed me back to Christ and a faithful God who never leaves us or forsakes us, especially during our darkest days. Our spunky Caroline Faith was born on October 28, 2010, and her little life brought great healing to my heart. Finally, on September 3, 2013, our little drummer boy Judah came along, and for a moment, we thought our family was complete. But God had other plans.

On October 15, 2017, I found myself standing in a foreign hotel room with Jeff and our two oldest children, Jonah and Ella, nervously gazing out the eighth story window. Skyscrapers surrounded us on every side, and there seemed to be hundreds of zooming mopeds on the busy streets below. It was a surreal moment. God had scheduled another divine appointment. It was about to take place in Fuzhou, China, where we would be meeting a nineteen-month-old little girl with Down syndrome who was about to become our daughter.

Before I share about the unforgettable day when we met Adeline, I want to give a little backstory about how we came to this place halfway across the world to grow our family through an international special needs adoption.

Jeff and I homeschool the kids, and we spent the 2015-2016 school year studying the lives of people who had devoted themselves to care for others and share the gospel around the world. We read missionary stories about Nate Saint, Amy Carmichael, Gladys Aylward, and one of our favorites, George Mueller. Stories of his faith, in particular, nudged and encouraged us as a family to go deeper in our walk with Christ. God used him in significant ways to care for the orphans in Bristol, England, during the 1800s. Reading the stories of God's provision in His life encouraged our faith so much. I love his words here: "Be assured if you walk with Him and look to Him, and expect help from Him, He will never fail you." We wanted this kind of faith; we craved it.

The idea of adoption began to surface from the depths of our hearts. Jeff and I couldn't shake it off. We talked about it constantly and started praying about the possibility for our family to adopt. We witnessed multiple friends walk the journey to adopt children domestically and from all over the world. Could God be calling our family to step out in faith and begin the process of growing our tribe of five kids to six through adoption? It was an easy sell for our kids, who were 100 percent on board. Their genuine, childlike faith was a beautiful thing to experience and an excellent source of encouragement for mom and dad! But, from what country would we adopt? Would it be a boy or a girl? How old will the child be? With so many questions, it was hard to know where to begin.

We contacted an agency, All God's Children International. We began to dialogue with them, and based on our family size and income, we realized we were able to adopt from Haiti, Burundi, Bulgaria, and China. Initially, we were ready to go back to Haiti, back to where it all began! However, looking at the timeline, the process looked like it would be a grueling four years of paperwork and waiting, at best. This wouldn't do, because we desired to adopt a child and have them home before Jonah left for college in 2020. So for now, the door closed on adopting from Haiti. But China kept coming back into our conversations, and after more talks and prayers, we began to go through the China program's sixty-four-page orientation packet.

Sitting at our social worker's desk for our initial home study interview, we walked through pretty much our whole life story and what had led us to this place. Near the end of the conversation, she began to review the special needs checklist we were required to fill out; after all, we chose to adopt a child with special needs. However, this was the part of the process that concerned us most. Wouldn't a child with special needs require so much more time and energy, not to mention financial obligations? Would our choice to adopt a "needy child" take away from our five children who already needed our constant love, time, and attention?

With me being a stay-at-home mom and Jeff in full-time ministry, we settled on keeping things manageable, so we checked only the things that were considered to be minor-to-correctable special needs. I guess you could say we were keeping it "safe." But safe faith? Faith requires trust and obedience that leads us out of our comfortable places, places where we feel we have some control. Wasn't our prayer for God to increase our faith? To quote our adoption fundraising t-shirts, we were praying for Him to give us "faith without borders." We struggled through this special needs checklist, and even after turning it back in to our social worker, were still conflicted and unsure of our decision.

But God, in His patient, long-suffering love for us, always guides us right where we need to be. He did this through a series of divine networking right before our eyes. In the early months of filling out paperwork, we also joined a China adoption Facebook group through our agency. A world opened to us that we had no idea even existed. As an adoptive family neared the time they would receive travel approval, they would invite people to join them on their journey to China through closed Facebook groups. We watched intently and admiringly as one family after another would go and meet their children.

We were drawn to one family in particular. They were from our home state of North Carolina, so maybe we just felt a little more kinship with them, but their journey to meet their son stirred something in us. We had seen this little boy on our agency's website, and now it was his family's turn to come for him!

Our hearts filled with hope, excitement, and awe as we watched this family, who had walked the same road we were starting on, meet their precious son, an orphan no more, who happened to have Down syndrome. We were drawn to learn more about children with Down syndrome in the Chinese orphanages.

What we learned shattered our hearts. According to our agency, their partner orphanage had 300 children living there, 100 of whom have Down syndrome. Many of these children never had a file made for them because it was assumed no one would ever choose to adopt a child with this particular need. Once a child turns fourteen, they are considered "aged out." They will go on to live in an institution for the rest of their days, an institution void of a mother's love and a father's guidance.

I couldn't stand the thought of a child, the same age as my oldest at the time, being taken away to live in this type of place. A place where they never felt loved or wanted. A place where they may never hear about their heavenly Father who created them and loves them unconditionally. Something needed to be done to encourage these orphanages to prepare files for these children living with Down syndrome. Who was going to step up? And, even if the files were processed, who would answer the call to bring these children home?

About half a year later, as we were driving to Charlotte to get our highly anticipated fingerprint appointment, we saw her photo. It was the very first photo we saw of her, the one where we knew this one was different. There was an immediate connection with her sweet little face; a glimpse of hope in her dark eyes. With guarded excitement, I told my husband, who was driving at the time, that he needed to see this little girl's photo. But, there's one thing he needed to know; this little one had Down syndrome.

At this point, Down syndrome was not included on the special needs checklist in our home study, which we had just completed the month before. There were so many unknowns, but by the time we reached the immigration building, I had already typed an email to our caseworker requesting little "Violet's" file. We received a quick reply that they did not have her completed file but would send us the information they did have on her as soon as possible.

We began to pray over this little one. For us, this was such a big decision to move forward with a child whose special need was considered neither "minor" nor "correctable." We reached out to friends who had adopted children with Down syndrome, we read blogs of families touched by Down syndrome, and we followed Instagram and Facebook accounts. We researched Down syndrome and tried to gain as much knowledge as possible to help us in our decision. We were softening to the possibility, but still, there were so many "what ifs."

Then her file came to us. I couldn't get her out of my mind. My heart tugged for her. I felt she was our daughter and the baby sister to our kids, but the fear of moving forward was real. How easy it would be to close the file and never open it again. We could move on, and who would judge us? It was at this time God eased our fear through the child-like faith of our children.

It is so sweet to us to see how God used the faith of our kids to encourage us to say "Yes" to bringing this precious one home to us. Jonah, fourteen at the time, took the time to think and pray about it. He came back to us a few days later, letting us know that God had given him peace about being this little child's big brother. Our girls couldn't stop talking about her, either. Every spare minute they would be drawing her pictures that they wanted to send to her. On February 22, 2017, which also happened to be her first birthday, we began the AOR process to bring her into our family, our sweet little Lian Anxin, whom we later named Adeline Hope.

As we continued the process, fear would resurface from time to time. At one point I felt stuck in our decision to adopt, and I begged God to relieve us of what felt like a life sentence of a burden to carry. I felt so inadequate. I began to stress out about how difficult our lives were going to be in the future. Everything felt bleak to me, as I pondered the sacrifices our family would be required to make once we added this child to our family. Being a mom to five is hard enough, and now we will have six, not to mention the unknowns that came along with her "designer genes."

My mind filled with worry and anxiety, and I lost a lot of sleep. Instead of seeking help and talking out my fears honestly, my pride began to take over, and I started to withdraw from friends and family. I put on a happy face as needed, but for the most part, I was scared to death but didn't want anyone to know it. Through the emotional turmoil and all the self-questioning, judging, and doubting, I ended up with a painful case of the shingles. God's word where He says, do not worry, be anxious for nothing, became my daily prayer.

I now know that God allowed me to go through this time of personal crisis to remind me of His faithfulness. I'm thankful that He helped me stay the course and not give up. He saw me through the daunting, helpless nights when I felt like it was just my tear-soaked pillow and I.

As I thought about our little one alone in a crib somewhere in China, He tenderly reminded me that I was His child, once lost and alone, and He had adopted me into His family. His grace, through the truth of His Word, brought me around again to embrace our calling to adopt. A precious calling that surpasses the here and now, it's truly a calling of eternal value, and He had invited us to join Him. If I had quit when I was the most scared, I would have missed out on the incredible miracle He was working in our family, and I would have kept the rest of my family from experiencing it, too.

Jeff and I feel strongly about leaving a legacy of faith in God to our children. There is nothing greater on earth for our kids to do than to put their trust in Christ. We want them to know He is faithful to His word, cares for us deeply, and is present in our daily lives. Whether we realize it or not, our kids are watching us; they have a front row seat to our lives, and the choices we make impact them. We want them to see their imperfect mom and dad doing their best to trust God and relying on Him day in and day out. We want them to experience God's nearness and how He genuinely cares for even the smallest details of our lives. As we were raising funds for our adoption, we knew the financial burden, in particular, could have kept us from moving forward, but we knew God had called us to this and He would provide what we needed.

At one point, the expenses were adding up and we needed $18,500, definitely not an amount we had in our bank account. We decided that we would spend time praying together as a family for one month, trusting God to provide in ways only He could. It was during that month that one of the girls from my high school small group informed me that her mom was a professional grant writer, and she wanted to help us apply for some adoption grants. Long story short, these grants were due on the last day of the month that we had committed to prayer. We applied for six grants and received funds from five of them totaling $18,500, the exact amount we had been praying for God to provide. Our kids still talk about how God heard our prayers and met this need to the penny! His nearness to us each day makes the challenging faith steps worth it. It's such a humbling experience when we can stop and recognize, "Wow, Emmanuel, God **is** with us, and He did that for us!"

When the day finally arrived to meet our daughter, we knew God had gone before us and was with us there. It was as if we were standing on holy ground. And then the moment came.

My heart was racing and tears filled my eyes as this tiny, dark-eyed cutie was carried into the stuffy conference room of the Kempinski Hotel. She was so small and timid, unsure of who we were and why she was there. The orphanage directors introduced us, and she immediately turned away from us. We were strangers to her, and as much as I desired for her to connect with us, I knew to be prepared for her to reject us completely.

We continued to speak softly to her, showing her toys and her soft blanket, and then, somewhat reluctantly, she came to me—my sweet Adeline. After months and months of prayers, tears, and mounds of paperwork, she was finally nestled in my arms. Her demeanor remained stoic at first, but little by little she let her guard down and relaxed in my embrace. Later that evening, as we were getting her ready for bed, she even shared her laughter with us; what we now fondly call Adeline's "kookaburra laugh!"

Our time in China with Adeline went very smoothly. She never outwardly grieved as far as we could tell; however, we were amazed at how she could put herself to sleep for naps and bedtime. We assumed she learned this from her foster mom. She wasn't interested in having me rock or cradle her; she just wanted me to lay her down and off she'd go to sleep. Two weeks went by, and before we knew it, we were boarding the plane in Guangzhou, China. Thirty exhausting hours later, we were being welcomed home in Charlotte, NC, by an excited group of family and friends.

Our homecoming to the States brought with it ups and downs as we transitioned from a family of seven to a family of eight. Our first morning home with all the kids felt like Christmas morning. We had nowhere to be, and we took advantage of this with everyone in PJs, sleepy-eyed, with luggage, laundry, and toys everywhere. The three kids who were meeting Adeline for the first time vied for her attention and were discouraged when she didn't seem too interested in them. Our four-year-old struggled the most and, at one point, asked when "that baby was going back to China."

We had to talk about giving grace and receiving grace from each other, a lot! The exhaustion and fatigue that came along with the jet lag caused emotions to rise, tempers to flare, and the walls of our home to cave in on us at times. Life just kept going, and our "real life" schedule and responsibilities came at us like a freight train. But again, grace for each day was available to us, and it has taught us much about being patient and forgiving with one another.

We have been on the other side of the adoption journey for just over eight months now. Our sweet, easygoing daughter has brought incredible joy to our family. She has amazed us with her ability to settle right in with our busy lives. We have seen her blossom before our eyes. She is walking now, feeding herself, and communicating with us by using sign language. She is beginning to turn on her voice and saying some words as well. Her bond with each of her siblings is a beautiful thing to witness, and they all adore her. She's mama's girl and daddy's little peanut.

I wish, when we first started out in the special needs adoption program, that my troubled heart could have rested more and feared the unknown less. I guess it gives me an opportunity and a platform to boast in my weaknesses, because God's power certainly has done a work in me. Even though we continue to find ourselves in the midst of fighting spiritual battles and overcoming obstacles, the hope we have in Christ far outweighs the costs and sacrifices we choose to make on a daily basis.

I would adopt a child with Down syndrome all over again. Our lives are better because of her, and it brings us so much joy to see the way she brings smiles and happiness to the people she meets. I love being able to encourage others who receive the nudge to adopt one of these precious children to step forward with confidence. First of all, these children are amazing and so worth it, but also because I know without a doubt that God's grace is sufficient.

CHAPTER
ELEVEN

worTH'S sTory

Just the other day, an acquaintance asked me how many children I have. As I opened my mouth to answer her, my words caught in my throat. Sometimes I wish there was an "it's complicated" box to check.

You see, I have one son. He is the only child who has ever lived in my home. But before him, there was a little girl named Wren. Although she and I never actually met, she was the magic and tragedy that completely changed my life.

I always knew I wanted to adopt. Throughout high school and college, I read blogs and followed the adoption journeys of countless families. I would picture my future family as a rainbow, filled with children from all parts of the world. I started seriously looking into that process in my early twenties. For several years, it always seemed that there was one more thing to do first, one more box to check, one more reason why adoption was not practical.

But unlike some ideas of my early twenties, this longing never faded. That's how I stumbled upon the Reece's Rainbow special needs orphan advocacy website. There I found pages and pages of tiny faces, tiny stories, tiny lives. I would stare for hours at sad eyes and starving bodies and wish that every face would soon see her mama.

I hurt for those forgotten ones, but I knew special needs adoption wasn't for me. Even as I cried tears of pain and joy with families I only knew through a screen, I didn't understand. I started looking into adoption, planning for a little girl with no special needs, and no older than two.

But then, special needs adoption smacked me in the face. I saw my child. I saw Wren, and I was changed. She wasn't just some kid around the world; she was mine. I felt her deep in my soul. She changed me.

But I'm getting ahead of myself; let's start at the beginning. I was twenty-five and single when I started seriously looking into adoption. I wanted to adopt from Africa.

After a series of events that seemed like "signs," I committed to adopting a little girl in an African country. I rushed to finish my home study and move forward with the process. Right around the time my home study was complete, I learned that this child's country was not going to allow me to proceed with her adoption. I had no idea what to do. This child needed a family. Or so I thought.

As I began to look past the rosiness of adoption, I was hit with some hard truths. Corruption. Ethics. Poverty. Family preservation. As I learned more about these topics and listened to the voices of those who had gone before me, I realized that adoption was not about me saving anyone. In fact, I strongly believe that such thinking is dangerous for everyone involved in the process. No matter how much I wanted to bring her home, I realized that my American family was not the best place for this African child.

With a head and heart full of more questions than answers, I decided to take a break from adoption. I was waiting for another sign that it was time to move forward.

And then one day as I scrolled mindlessly on Facebook, I saw a picture and my world was flipped upside down. Staring at me through the screen were the sunken, almond-shaped eyes and hollow cheeks of a tiny child; it was obvious that she was starving. I quickly skimmed the blurb accompanying her haunting picture to learn that this infant-sized child was actually five years old. This little girl, named "Heavenleigh" by the advocacy website, was born with Down syndrome.

After the initial shock, my first thought was, "Her mama needs to find her. Fast." I said a little prayer for her and continued on with my day. As her picture gained traction on social media, I repeated my plea, "Mama, see her. God, send her family **soon**."

I couldn't stop thinking about the tiny girl in the pink sleeper. I couldn't stop thinking about the five years of neglect. Five years without a mama and goodnight kisses. Five years of silent pain.

And then, while still praying for her family to come soon, I emailed her agency. I quickly received a return email saying that she was in Bulgaria, a country that was very open to single moms. They sent me new pictures and videos of this little girl. With tears in my eyes, I studied each one. I could see this little girl's ribs. Her socks were too loose on her ankles. She sucked on her tongue and smiled as she tried to figure out the rattle they placed awkwardly in her hand.

As I continued to pore over her pictures and medical information, the question in my mind slowly shifted from, *Where is her family?* to *Could I be her family?* to *How could I not?*

And then, I knew. It wasn't some miraculous sign that led me to say "Yes." I did not search for a starving child or a child with Down syndrome. Instead, it was the realization that this child desperately needed a family, and I was a family. I was a ready and willing "Yes."

This tiny girl in the pink sleeper was waiting for someone. By no fault of her own, international adoption had become her only option for a future.

I named her "Wren"; a tiny bird. She had been caged for far too long, but she would soon be free. She would be a beloved daughter.

In my blog post announcing my commitment to Heavenleigh, I wrote: "She has made it for five years; I believe she can make it a few more months." I had no idea as I typed those words just how right they would be.

On Monday, November 9, 2015, I got a phone call that changed my life. Wren was no longer alive on earth.

I remember hearing the words through the phone and not being able to breathe. It was as if time just stopped and if I didn't inhale, maybe it wouldn't be true; maybe she was still breathing. I didn't know what to say. How do you react to the news that your child is gone?

I had absolutely no idea how to move forward, but at the same time, a new fire was ignited in my heart. My abstract commitment to children being in families now had real ramifications. Without families, children die.

Even though her life was short and confined to a crib, Wren was a world changer. Thousands of people saw the pictures of a tiny, broken girl now made whole. Thousands of people know more about the injustices of this world because of one tiny girl in a pink sleeper.

When I found out about Wren's death, my heart shattered. It felt like it could never hold love again because the love would just run out of all the brokenness. As the reality of Wren's death set in, I realized that I had two choices. I could walk away from adoption or I could catch my breath and carry on. My heart was truly shattered, but I had to remember that adoption wasn't about my comfort zone. In all of my adventures, I have found that the greatest joy and the most breathtaking views are found outside of your comfort zone. Adoption is no different. I do not for one second regret saying "Yes."

One day, a few weeks before Wren passed away, I noticed a little boy on Reece's Rainbow I had never seen before. It was his hair that caught my eye; it was blonde and wispy and reminded me of my dad.

He had Down syndrome, just like Wren, and he, too, was waiting in Bulgaria. His smile lit up his face, and in some profound way, I felt connected to him. For a brief minute, I thought about adding him to my adoption of Wren, but I knew that Wren's needs were too intense, and even if it was possible, I couldn't risk delaying things for Wren. I thought, *Sweet boy, if you are still waiting in a year or so, I'll come back for you. (But please don't let him still be waiting in a year!)*

It was as though, somehow, I caught a little glimpse of what the future held. Wren was gone, but her life gave meaning to the passion within me. Just a few months before seeing her picture, adopting a child with Down syndrome was not on my radar. In fact, I thought special needs were scary. I simply wasn't equipped. One of the miracles of Wren's short life was the radical change in perception she gave me. When I saw her picture, it wasn't a list of diagnoses that I saw; I saw a child who needed a family. She showed me a simplicity I had never experienced.

I emailed my agency to ask about the little boy with the wispy blonde hair. By some miracle, they already had his file and would hold on to it for a few more weeks. They sent me his medical records, along with several videos. I learned that he was almost nine years old but the size of a toddler. He had recently learned to walk and, by the wide smiles in the videos, was very proud of that. He made all kinds of expressive faces, he had open-heart surgery right after his second birthday, and he was unimpressed with the toys in the playroom.

With a handful of notarized documents and a few updates to my home study, I was officially committed to adopting this little boy. The darkest nights in my adoption journey led to a beautiful dawn.

In May of 2016, I got the green light from Bulgaria to travel to meet the little boy I had named Worth Allen. The anticipation was unlike anything I have ever experienced. As I flew around the world to become a mother for the first time, my arms were suddenly hyper-aware of their emptiness. So many questions about the one who would fill them constantly ran through my head. I was able to sleep only in little bursts.

And then it was time. It was a Monday morning in Sofia, the capital of Bulgaria. It had been raining all night but was only drizzling when I left the hotel with my translator. We took a cab ride through the grey city streets, and all I could think about was seeing him for the first time. Would I recognize him? Would he cry? Would a nanny hover over us as we got to know each other?

The cab pulled up to a nice little two-story building. It was fenced in with a playground in the front. This was it. My son was here. My heart was pounding in my ears; I was sure others could hear it too.

I focused my nervousness on avoiding puddles as we walked through the gate, then the front door. A friendly woman greeted us, and then took us to the adjacent building. Again, I concentrated on the puddles.

We walked into a room where I saw three or four children, older children. One girl rolled up to me in her wheelchair and pulled on my backpack strap. I smiled at her as I scanned the room.

The friendly lady reached down into a pack-and-play I had not noticed before. She pulled out a tiny little boy in a blue tracksuit. I saw his blonde hair and knew it was him. As she put him onto her hip, I smiled and reached for him, more out of instinct than conscious movement.

And he reached out his tiny arms for me. I held him for the first time, and stroked his hair. He was so small and so perfect. This moment was so long awaited; the child I had loved for months through the screen of a computer was now in my arms.

We were whisked away into a playroom where a nurse was eager for me to see his skills. He walked. He climbed out of the ball pit. He loved to clap his hands. I *oohed* and *aahed* at each accomplishment, but really, he could have done none of that and still been just as much mine. Every time he was out of my arms, he tottered back to me with a silly grin.

As the first visit came to a close, I carried Worth downstairs and handed him to a nanny who swiftly placed him back into the pack-and-play. Each time I entered the orphanage, he was sitting there, silently waiting. Each time I left, he was returned to his crib.

On the afternoon of my second day of visiting, the nanny brought Worth to me with a fresh cut on his forehead. It took a moment to register, but I realized it was from repeatedly banging his head on the side of a crib.

"He doesn't like to nap," the nanny explained calmly, ignoring the horror that undoubtedly seeped through my attempt at composure.

As my week of getting to know Worth came to an end, the thought of leaving him in that orphanage to spend his days alone in a pack-and-play made me feel sick. On our last afternoon together, I held him close and promised over and over that I would be back as soon as I could.

When I carried him down the stairs for the last time, I could barely see past the tears in my eyes. I had to leave and allow the adoption process to proceed. I had to go home so that I could come back. I knew, but that didn't make it any easier.

I kissed his scarred little forehead and told him how loved he was. I could only pray that somehow my words would carry us both until we were together again.

For the next few months, I stayed as busy as I could in hopes of rushing time along. There was more paperwork, more fingerprints, and more medical checks. Amid the business and the waiting, my life changed again.

In the summer of 2016, as I waited to bring my son home, I joined an online dating site. I was looking for someone to go kayaking with me, but somehow I found so much more (and he still owes me a kayaking trip). When Chris and I connected, he told me about his puppy and his love of hockey, and I told him about my son on the other side of the world. I fully expected him to wish me all the best and move on, but instead, he asked me on a date.

He was standing in the parking lot of the bowling alley, waiting for me, when I pulled in. I knew from the moment I saw him there waving at me that I had stumbled upon something special. One date turned into two; dates turned into dinner together every night. He asked to see pictures and videos of the little boy who held my heart. He shopped for diapers and tiny clothes with me. He offered to try out the baby food to make sure it was good enough.

On September 16, 2016, a judge in Sofia, Bulgaria, officially made me the mom of Worth Allen. He was awarded all the rights and privileges of a child born from my womb. He received my last name. He had no idea how his life was about to change. I began making plans to travel back to Bulgaria and, this time, come home with a son.

Just a week before the trip and in the midst of the beautiful chaos of preparing to be a parent, Chris took me back to the bowling alley where we had our first date. I bowled my first strike and turned back to see him down on one knee with my grandmother's ring in his hand. He asked me to be his wife, and promised to love my son and me forever. I said, "Yes."

Chris and I traveled together to Bulgaria to carry Worth out of his orphanage and into his forever family. It had been five months since I walked out of those orphanage doors with empty arms. Would Worth remember me? How would he react to life outside of those walls?

Once again, Sofia was blanketed in grey clouds. The drive through the city streets was silent; my heart was racing as I watched for the familiar buildings that held my son. Soon, we were stepping out of the car and walking through those gates. I scanned each room for my son. We were taken up the stairs to a small room with a large table and several women. Our translator discussed paperwork with the woman I assumed was the director, and Chris and I were shown to our assigned chairs at the table.

And then we saw Worth. I wanted to jump up and run to him, but at this point, the room was full of people, and I could see he was already unsure of his surroundings. Women stooped down to hug and kiss him as he held onto the hands of a young girl, the daughter of one of the nannies.

Finally, the papers were signed; I could wait no longer. Worth was back in my arms, and I let out a breath I didn't realize I was holding. We walked down those familiar stairs and back out through the small playground. I waved goodbye and thanked the only people my son ever knew.

As I carried my tiny boy out through those gates, the magnitude of the moment struck me. The little boy in my arms had spent 3,583 days as an orphan, removed from his society because of his extra chromosome. On this day, he became a son whose very name forced the world to recognize his value, his Worth. He could no longer be overlooked; he was forever grafted into our family tree.

On the ride back to the hotel, Worth sat in silence, his tiny hand holding Chris's strong one. My eyes filled with tears as I watched these two enter each other's lives; it was as if Worth knew he could trust his new Daddy to protect him in this uncharted territory.

For the next few days, Worth spent his time sitting silently. He did not try to explore; he did not move unless one of us took him by the hand. He sat glued to the last place we put him. When we fed him, he kept his hands folded tight in his lap. He wouldn't touch food. After much coaxing, he allowed us to place his hand in ours as we spoon-fed him soft foods. He didn't know how to chew or drink liquids; we were thankful for friends who had gone before us because they were able to suggest special bottles we could use to squirt small amounts of water or milk into his mouth.

With each passing day in that Bulgarian hotel, Worth opened his shell little by little. We caught glimpses of his sass. We laughed as he smiled at himself in the mirrored walls of the elevator. We cheered him on as he took more and more steps independently before becoming too tired.

And as we got home and settled in, the milestones continued. Things that most people would not think about twice were cause for joyous celebrations. Worth attempted to spoon-feed himself. He learned to stand up from sitting on the ground. He found a favorite toy and quickly figured out how to push the button until it cycled to his favorite song. Worth came to life before our eyes.

A few weeks after coming home, Worth was admitted to the hospital to watch for refeeding syndrome. Because his body had learned to live off of so few calories for so many years, we had to increase his intake slowly so as not to shock his system. A naso-gastric tube was placed from his nose into his stomach so that we could safely feed him while working to improve his strength and coordination to eat by mouth.

Eventually, we had a gastric tube surgically placed in Worth's stomach. This allows us to supplement his calories as needed and ensures that he gets enough water. His ability to drink has dramatically improved from those first weeks home, but he still struggles.

On December 31, 2016, Chris and I were married on a bridge overlooking our city. We promised to love each other and our son and to continue to build a longer table. Our prayer as a couple on that day and always is that our love be so abundant that we have plenty to share with the world.

Each day is an opportunity for a new adventure for Worth. He continually amazes us with his joyful spirit and tenacity. Beyond his physical development and growth, Worth has learned what it means to have a family. He no longer allows just anyone to hold or hug him. He seeks out comfort from his mom and dad. He knows that his place in this family is permanent; he is securely attached. Beyond any ability or talent, Worth's learned sense of security is my biggest joy.

Wren taught me that love can't come a day too soon. Worth showed me the redemption and broken joy of boldly living out that love.

Adoption is beautiful, but that beauty comes at a high cost for all involved. The very essence of adoption is born from the greatest loss one can experience—the loss of family. This trauma, whether from day one or day three thousand and one, changes our children's brains. Although the love of a family is redemptive, it cannot undo trauma. We, as parents of adopted children, must always remember that adoption is a promise we make and must uphold daily to help our children grow and heal.

To those considering special needs adoption, my advice is to jump in with eyes wide open. Listen to those who have walked this road before you. Meet children from hard places. Read the research. Expect to be tested like never before. Love and accept the child you have, not the idealized child you hoped for or the child you see on someone else's social media. Celebrate tiny glimpses of growth; celebrate your child for who they are, not how they compare to others.

Above all, love big. Love boldly. And love always, even when it's not easy.

Orphans don't need saving. They need families. They need moms and dads who are willing to open their homes to the messiness and joy of the unknown. They need people willing to take chances and see past a list of diagnoses. They need fierce love and security, through the fears and newness of being vulnerable to love.

Children belong in families. This I will shout until my dying day; this I hope to leave as my legacy.

CHAPTER
TWELVE

LUCY, HENRY, AND ELOISE'S STORY

If you had told me twenty years ago this would be my life, I would not have believed you. We are expecting our ninth child, have adopted three special needs children from China, and have two daughters with Down syndrome. This is not the easy, comfortable life that I would have imagined. To understand our story, what we refer to as *A Real Life Fairytale*, we must go back to the beginning where it all began...

My husband, Brent, and I started dating when I was fifteen. By the time I was entering college, my biggest desire was to be a wife and mom. I had grown up an only child, and the loneliness of a house without siblings and playmates had left me longing for a home with children, and lots of them! As a child, I spent most of my time talking to my dolls and playing alone in my room or outside under a tree. I believe this time to myself built a security in me, an acceptance of being by myself and not relying on others to bring happiness. It also created a need I have to retreat and be in solitude. Looking back, the decision my parents made when I was nine years old may have had the most significant impact on my life, and only just recently was I able to identify it.

When I was a young girl, around fourth grade, my parents were trying to conceive a child. Unable to do so, they turned to adoption. I have only a vague memory of the process now, but I remember being told I was getting a sibling, and within a few months we were driving to the hospital to meet my newborn baby brother.

Adoption had been presented to me in such an accepted, normal, even common way that in those formative years I never regarded it as being an unusual or exceptional way of growing a family. It was quite simply, in my mind, just another way of having a child.

As my baby brother grew, I became his protective caregiver; we didn't have the usual brother/sister relationship. I spent hours reading to him and rocking him and investing in his little life. Even though he had blond hair and blue eyes that contrasted with my dark hair and green eyes, it never occurred to me to lessen the bond we shared. I believe this fundamentally shaped my ideas about adoption.

High school was an awkward time for me. I had my boyfriend (who would become my husband), but I am by nature an introvert. I can clearly remember two distinct events from my years as a teenager that shaped my path to becoming a mother to orphans. The first was the realization of the one-child policy in China. I heard somewhere about that policy creating an orphan epidemic in China, and then I did all the reading and researching I could on the subject.

It fascinated me that a policy meant to help the people of a country battling starvation and overpopulation could lead to the infanticide of millions of baby girls, and still more were abandoned and growing up in orphanages. I vowed—after reading a story of a young mother leaving her baby daughter under the seat on a train and then dashing out of sight before the authorities could catch her—that one day I would do whatever I could to be a mother to the motherless. My heart bled and grieved with the mothers making the painful choice of giving up their children.

Around this same time, a groundbreaking movie was released; it was about the plight of a man in Nazi Germany working tirelessly to save the lives of Jews during the Holocaust. *Schindler's List* culminated in a scene where Schindler had sacrificed all that he had and yet, in desperation, takes off his watch and ring, crying out, "These could have saved just one more!" Although it's been twenty-four years since I first heard those words, the impact of their meaning still stirs me today. I don't want to look back on my life as I near the end and cry out, "I could have saved one more, but I chose not to."

The culmination of adoption in my personal life, my connection to the mothers of China, and the thought of living a life that was not fully spent at the end led me to a deep conviction that I shared with my husband from the beginning of our marriage. Although he had not shared in the same experiences leading me to this path, he agreed to pursue whatever I felt passionate about.

Soon after our wedding, Brent began medical school, and we became pregnant with our first child. The joy I felt over becoming a mother was indescribable. Thirteen months later we found out we were expecting again, and two years after that we were pregnant for the third time. Our hands were full with three little ones and the medical residency, but our hearts were so full also. We decided at the time that our family was complete. But we would learn over the years that just when we thought our plans were the best, God had something else in store for us.

The thoughts of adoption and children in need of families still haunted me. When our youngest was around six years of age, through prayer and support from our church family, we decided to pursue our first adoption. We started by contacting an agency that worked exclusively with China adoptions. But when we requested we be matched with a baby boy, the conversation quickly led us to agencies that worked with other countries where male adoptions were available.

Our hearts were set on China; however, we felt a strong guidance from the Lord that our next child would be a boy. While working to complete our home study, we learned we were, indeed, pregnant again. The country we were working to adopt from, Ethiopia, did not allow a smaller gap than eighteen months between biological and adopted children. Our adoption was put on hold, and we gave birth to our fourth child, a boy.

Two years later, much to our surprise, we had our fifth child, a feisty and energetic little girl. Again, we considered our hands full and our family complete. All conversations of adoption were over, and we focused our attention on raising our teenagers and preschoolers to the best of our ability. But in late January of 2015, God had other plans. He was preparing our hearts for what would become the biggest and wildest ride of our lives. He was using the story of a little orphan with Down syndrome in China to stir something bigger in us, and eventually in the world. He wanted to make His goodness and love known to many, and He would accomplish it through the most unlikely of participants; our family.

There are a handful of days in one's life that you never forget. The day you say "I do," the birth of a child and, for me, the day I first laid eyes on my daughter. A two by two picture with a number instead of a name, but I knew without a shadow of a doubt that it was the face of my child.

The adoption agency that we had contacted eight years earlier had sent my husband an email at his work. This was the first and only contact we had with them in almost a decade, and we were in no way entertaining the thought of adoption. The door had closed on us many times before and we were enjoying a relatively smooth and comfortable life. Five children were more than enough for our busy family.

After reading the email over a quick lunch break, Brent made the fateful decision to forward it to my email. The agency was looking for families to volunteer to take an orphan from China into their home for the summer and advocate for a family for them. All the children eligible for the program had to be over six years old and deemed hard to place. I had never heard of such a program and was so intrigued by the idea of hosting an orphan. Even more intriguing was that my husband had willingly forwarded it to me. I felt that if we were never going to adopt a child, we could, at least, give one summer to let a child experience what a family means.

I opened the website with the photos of the children who had made the list, with butterflies inside my stomach. There were approximately one hundred kids with bios, and only the first thirty to be selected would get to make the trip for the summer.

As I scrolled through the photos of each child, I prayed, "Lord, if you are asking us to do this, to bring a child into our family for the summer, please tell me which one to choose." I felt ashamed, looking at the pictures of children without parents and then continuing to scroll down. The enormity of what I was actually choosing was so heavy that it was almost too much for me. Who was I to say that one child was more desirable than another, when I knew that for thirty kids who were lucky enough to be chosen, this was their only ticket to belonging to a family?

After closing my computer and taking the rest of the day to pray, I finally opened the website again. This time I landed on a picture of a little girl dressed in a red coat with a short black bob haircut who was listed as C 15-20. In her description box, she had been nicknamed "Miss Tickles."

My heart stopped beating, and for a moment, I felt all the blood leave my head. Without any warning or thought, I began weeping. The voice of the Holy Spirit told me I was looking at the face of my daughter. There was something else in her description that was a huge issue. She had Down syndrome.

To many new parents, getting a prenatal diagnosis of Down syndrome brings grief and sadness. More than 90 percent of mothers decide to abort their child with Down syndrome, rather than carry the baby to term. For me, the people in my life with Down syndrome had given me a different perspective than most.

From the time I was in junior high, I would see a child or adult with Down syndrome and would have a feeling deep in my soul that I would one day have a baby with Down syndrome. The feeling became so strong that it was inescapable. I distinctly remember being on a high school trip where we saw a young man with Down syndrome playing a guitar for money. I knew, looking into his eyes, that this would be my path in life. It was not as if I ever felt, *I hope I have a child with Down syndrome*, it was a feeling inside me that simply stated, *You are going to have a child with Down syndrome.*

When my husband and I became pregnant with our first child, I knew this bit of information was something I had to share with him. He was not shaken or surprised about this secret I had been holding in my heart for years; he responded then as he always does. If the Lord sends something our way, He will also give us peace about it.

By the time we were pregnant with our fifth child, I was well into my mid-thirties. With each pregnancy, I held my breath when the doctor would give the news whether my unborn baby was "healthy" or "not healthy." So, by the fifth pregnancy, I knew without a doubt this child would be born with Down syndrome. My doctor did a screening for genetic markers at about fifteen weeks, and I remember the spot in my son's bedroom where I was standing when the phone rang from the doctor's office. They called to tell me my test results were back and that we were having a healthy girl with no genetic abnormalities.

I was shocked and confused; why would God be preparing my heart all these years to accept a baby with Down syndrome and then never fulfill it? I shared my thoughts with my husband, but his stance was always the same; if God gave us a child with Down syndrome, then it was meant to be, but it was not something he would pursue.

Years later, seeing the picture of our daughter known as C 15-20, I knew instantly that she was indeed what my heart had been prepared for. The Lord was not telling me that a child from my womb would have Down syndrome; He was molding and softening me to the point where I could say "Yes" to a child born to another woman, on the other side of the world, who was in desperate need of a family. He needed me to notice her, because He wanted to reach so many for His glory through her.

I shut my computer, and with shaky hands and tearful eyes, I sent a text to my husband at work. It said, "Go to the website and look up C 15-20." After a few moments, his response was, "I think she's our girl."

I knew he could not have possibly read her bio or looked too closely at her picture. He would have never said "Yes" to a special need so severe, so permanent, as Down syndrome. But he had read it. And he had agreed to host her. The only problem was, I was unwilling to host a child I felt was our daughter and then send her back to China forever without adopting her into our family. It took a few weeks, lots of prayer, and something in his heart changing, but by March of 2015, we were neck deep in adoption paperwork for the little girl we had named "Lucy."

The wait was a long five months until finally, one hot and humid day in July, thirty children stepped off a Chinese airplane and onto American soil. We were waiting at the gate along with all the other families hosting children, and there was a slew of news reporters and cameras there to capture the moment for the nightly news. Our adoption agency had given them a call in an effort to get the kids on television and increase their chances of a family seeing them and stepping forward to adopt. We had no idea at the time that the reporter choosing to focus on our family would ultimately send the headlines, "Special-needs orphan meets her Momma for the first time," literally around the world.

Meeting Lucy for the first time was the fulfillment of years of praying for this child. A child born of another womb on the other side of the world whom God would carry like a leaf in the wind until she landed safely in my arms forever. As I waited, watching expectantly as each person came through the gate, I was overcome with emotion. This child was an orphan on that airplane and within moments would become a cherished daughter. Her wait was about to be over.

I was finally living my dream too, a dream that was placed in my heart by a gracious God over twenty years ago. I was doing something to make a difference to the least of these. Our worlds, our hopes, our destinies were about to collide, and inside my heart, I was singing praises to the One who had designed it all. I knew my love for Lucy was unwavering, but I had no idea what her reaction to meeting me would be. Would she be scared by all the chaos at the airport? Would she be exhausted from the twenty-hour trip and fall apart?

When she came bouncing out of those airport doors, a smile stretched across her face, I couldn't hold back any longer. I dashed towards my daughter, bent down to look into her eyes, and said; "I am your mama."

Leaning into me, she whispered in confirmation, "Mama." In that moment, we were family. Not only had she accepted me, but she wouldn't let go of me! She wrapped her little arms around my neck and didn't let go for thirty minutes. She continued to periodically stare into my eyes and whisper, "Mama," as if checking to see if it was a dream. Over the next five weeks, Lucy would call me "Mama" hundreds of times a day. She would fall asleep lying on my chest, face pressed against mine, repeating in her soft, raspy voice, "Mama,

Mama." It was as if she had bottled up that simple word for six years and now she could finally use it—she had her own mama.

There was another word Lucy would always say: "Hao-wa!" It was always followed by a huge belly laugh. When we talked to people familiar with Chinese, it became clear she was saying a made-up version of the word "good." We called the translator (which is also Lucy's orphanage teacher, Ms. Liu) and asked what she was saying. Liu said she was copying her best friend, a little boy who is blind. We pondered for a moment... her best friend was a boy. And he was blind. Since we knew almost nothing about her life in China, every bit of information was a treasure to us.

We soaked in five weeks of love and bonding with Lucy. When the time had come for the hosting program to be over, all our hearts were breaking. I had tried everything in my power to keep her here. I had called my congressman. My husband called the ambassador to China. We pleaded with our agency to extend her visa and let her stay until her adoption papers were finalized. No one would budge. The rules of the hosting program were firm; Lucy must go back to the orphanage and wait for us to come to China and get her. We packed her suitcase and added some toys for the other children in her foster home. I made her a photo album with pictures of her time with us and of all the members of our family. All eight of us piled onto my bed and hugged, kissed, cried, and prayed before departing for the airport. It was gut-wrenching.

That could easily have been the end of the story. However, after Lucy left to go back to China, Brent told me a secret he had been keeping. He couldn't get the thought of the little blind boy out of his mind. He had been praying about what this meant and had come to the conclusion we should make him our son.

At first, I was shocked. I hadn't planned on adopting again... so soon. And I hadn't given a thought about Lucy's best friend. Furthermore, blindness was a special need that I hadn't checked on the list. But God has a way even when we don't see a way. He had a perfect plan for this little boy, and all He needed was for us to step out in one small step of faith and rely on Him to prepare the path. Isn't that the way God is? He takes us to a place of complete fear and uncertainty and then asks us to take the leap.

The next morning we were able to track down his file. All we had to go on was his orphanage and his name; Henry. We had made up our minds to adopt him before we saw his picture, knew his age, or read his medical file! The adoption agency warned us that he might never have had a file made. Even if he had, if another adoption agency was holding it, then we would not be able to adopt him with Lucy. But we knew that if this was the Lord's will, our son's file would be waiting for us. A call back just a few hours later confirmed that God had planted another orphan with our family.

In January of 2016, on a freezing cold day in Hunan, China, we left our hotel to take the drive to the Civil Affairs Office where we would be reunited with Lucy and meet our new son. We were as prepared as we could be, but when those doors opened we were caught so off guard we didn't even have our cameras out. Lucy entered the room first, put her hands on her hips, and with a big grin, said, in English, "What, baby?"

She had remembered that during her hosting trip she would continually ask, "Mama?" and I would always answer, "What, baby?" That sweet girl had been waiting six months to say to me, "What, baby?"

The honeymoon period continued with Lucy. She was happy, content, and seemed to attach to us so seamlessly that it felt she had always been a part of our family. Before leaving Hunan, we wanted to spend the day at her orphanage, to meet the nannies and foster parents that had raised her for the first six years. I also wanted to give the foster mom and dad a special gift to thank them for all they had done to care for Lucy and Henry. They agreed to meet with us and led us back to a small three-bedroom apartment in the center of the orphanage. Their foster mom greeted us at the door, and several foster siblings were in the living room. The main living area had a tile floor and hardwood furniture. There was a flat-screen television on the wall that Henry used to stand in front of and watch all day long.

Two boys, both with cerebral palsy, were in wheelchairs. A baby girl was standing up, holding onto the edge of the coffee table, not yet old enough to walk. She turned her head and looked at me, and my heart immediately melted. I walked over and picked her up. She looked like a younger version of Lucy, a tiny little girl with Down syndrome. As I turned around, I noticed my husband was taking pictures of us together.

I carried this little bundle around as we toured the bedrooms, and foster mom showed us the bed that Lucy and this baby had been sharing. She showed us the wall above the sofa where she proudly displayed a huge canvas photo of her and foster dad along with their foster children, including Lucy, Henry, and the baby I was holding. It was time to give the foster parents their gifts—for foster dad, a tee shirt from the Houston Rockets player Yao Ming, and for foster mom, a silver heart locket.

I asked our translator to tell her I was so grateful for all the love she had given Lucy and Henry and that she truly was their mother in every sense of the word. It was time to leave and continue on our tour of the orphanage, so I reluctantly propped the baby back at the corner of the coffee table and walked out the door. Having to turn my back to her, knowing that she would probably never have a family, just broke my heart. When we returned to our hotel that evening, I blogged about our day. I added the pictures Brent had taken of the baby and me, and I wrote these words:

"I know you have a mama out there. I am going to find her."

In May of 2017, it had been almost a year and a half since Lucy and Henry had come home. We had settled into a routine, and Lucy continued to bring our family so much joy. I decided to home-school Lucy, after a trial run at a private school that wasn't a good fit for her needs. Out of all seven of our children, Lucy was the easiest. Her simplicity, her joy, her loving nature was what our family needed in such a busy and chaotic season of life. She slowed us down and helped all of us keep perspective of what was most important in life.

We had once again decided that our family was complete. One night after everyone in the house had gone to bed, I was still up in the living room working on my laptop. I had not visited any websites advocating for orphan children since before adopting Lucy and Henry. Something inside my heart nudged me to look again. As I sat in the dark, I told the Lord that if He was calling us to adopt again, He would have to drop a child out of the sky into my lap. I hesitantly scrolled through a website advocating for children in China. There are almost one million orphans in China and thousands of orphanages scattered among the twenty-three provinces. One tiny picture caught my eye—one child out of the many.

In the comments section was a link to a video. Curious, I clicked on the video. There on the screen was a toddler dressed in a green jog suit with a birthday hat on, dancing around the room. I immediately recognized the cold tile floor and hardwood furniture. It was Lucy and Henry's living room. Then a woman appeared in view behind the child; she was wearing a Houston Rockets Yao Ming shirt and had a silver heart locket around her neck. It had been a year and a half since we were in China.

As I focused on the child in the video again, I realized it was her—the baby I had held a year earlier. Lucy's little foster sister. All I could think of was how impossible it would be that the first time I went on a website, I would open a video of the same little girl from Lucy and Henry's foster family inside their living room with my children's foster mother wearing the gifts I had given her. *Out of a million orphans in China.*

With tears in my eyes, I ran to the bedroom and woke Brent. I asked him to watch the video, which he did, but we had already agreed that our family was complete. We also knew in our hearts that we could not ignore the signs that God had given us, pointing us to this little girl. We put the decision on hold to pray about it. Several months went by.

Around the same time, China had tightened up the rules regarding international adoption. Families could no longer adopt two children at the same time as we had done before. Families that had a child at home under three years old could no longer adopt. And families with five children living at home were no longer able to adopt. We realized our family would be disqualified.

We were disheartened. We knew God had clearly given us a calling for this little girl, and because of our uncertainty, we had delayed.

Now we were no longer eligible to adopt her or any other child from China. If we had acted sooner, we would have been grandfathered in before the new rules were in effect. Additionally, two different families had moved forward with paperwork for this little girl who had been given the name "Quinn" on the advocacy sites. We were excited for Quinn, but we still felt we had missed God's plan. One by one, both families found out they were not eligible. Knowing we were not eligible either, we were heartbroken for little Quinn. Had our hesitancy kept her from her forever family?

A week or so later, I received a message from a good friend in the middle of the night. Her message was short and sweet: "Go get your little girl." She had learned that we had been misinterpreting the new rules. We could have up to five children living at home and still be eligible. Because our oldest child was living in another state and had her own apartment while going to college, and our second oldest was living in Europe enjoying a gap year after graduating high school a year early, we had only five children living at home. The new rules that we thought made us ineligible were actually what made us the only family eligible.

On July 20 we signed with our agency to adopt little Quinn, and only four months later, on November 17, we mailed our dossier to China! Exactly eight months after we first signed our adoption paperwork to start the process—on March 19, 2018—our new daughter, Eloise Mei Shook, was placed in our arms.

God's stories are always the *best* stories.

CHAPTER

THIRTEEN

minLan anD
jOHn preston's story

My husband, Bryan, and I have been married for twenty years. When we were dating, I told him that I wanted to adopt. As any loving boyfriend would, he agreed wholeheartedly with my ambitious dream. He didn't run away when he learned adoption was on my list. And not just any adoption; I wanted to adopt a child with Down syndrome.

Growing up, my husband and I had very different childhoods. He was the son of a father in retail, so they relocated frequently. No sooner had he settled in at a school and begun to make new friends than his father took a new job and the family moved yet again. He had one little sister and lived a pretty typical middle-class American life. Bryan's friends were the kids next door. They were all just worried about having enough daylight to ride their bikes down the big hill in the neighborhood one more time before their mother called them to dinner. When Bryan saw his friends, it was like looking at his own reflection in the mirror. Sameness.

I came home from the hospital to the little yellow-sided house that my parents still call home. I had many of the same friends from birth through graduation and into adulthood. I never knew the stress of packing all my belongings to move to another state, let alone having to start over and make new friends. My childhood was uneventful, as I recollect, and it all seemed so ordinary to me at the time.

Our family was complete after adding a little brother, Joshua, and a little sister, Jamie. My brother was four years my junior and diagnosed with cerebral palsy as an infant. Life with Joshua was the norm for us. Wheelchairs, special education classes, surgeries, and therapies didn't seem out of the ordinary. Being in a multi-handicap class before the days of inclusion meant friends with all levels of ability. Friends with varying special needs. Friends with Down syndrome.

I remember going to the Special Olympics with my brother. I remember seeing him celebrated. That was our life, growing up. Celebrating who my brother was. Never ashamed, never defeated. Just thankful. Thankful that the Lord had blessed our family with the gift of my brother.

That gift planted a desire in my heart—a desire to one day parent a child with special needs. For many years, I was unsure of how that would come to pass. It wouldn't be long before God revealed the plan that only He could orchestrate. My husband, blinded by new love, had agreed to my dream of adoption. Little did he know what was just around the corner…

When Bryan and I met, he had two precious little boys, and I became an instant parent. I was ready; maybe a little naive, but ready. I had always wanted to be a mother, so I jumped in wholeheartedly. As we learned to navigate the joys and heartache of a blended family, my heart was longing to hold a newborn of my very own and to hear the babble of a baby calling me "Momma." Years went by—six, to be exact—before I would hold our first daughter in my arms. I thought the day would never come. Ellie's birth was followed almost three years later by our son Ethan. Another two years passed quickly, and we welcomed our Ruby Kate. I had what I had always dreamed of; my very own family.

It wasn't long before that dream of adoption began to pull at my heart again. With three little ones at home, our days were busy and messy but still open to new possibilities. Having looked into international adoption, the financial piece of the puzzle was daunting. I could not see a way for that to be possible for our family. It seemed as though my dream was never going to become a reality.

The next logical step was to consider the local possibilities. I contacted our local Department of Human Resources, and they mailed us a packet of paperwork. Maybe being foster parents would lead to adoption. Maybe being open to fostering would somehow connect us with a local child with Down syndrome who needed a family. My dream was big and maybe a tad bit unrealistic, but my heart was not ready to give up on my dream just yet. I knew God had planted the desire in my heart. And even though I couldn't see it at the time, He was working. I just had to trust.

While I was anxious to start the process, Bryan began to express reservations. He was unsure of his ability to parent a child with special needs. Bryan confessed that he had never met a person with Down syndrome and wasn't sure if this was the right plan for our family. That dream of mine he had so willingly supported during our months of dating seemed to be further and further away. I didn't know how to move forward. I didn't want to push a reluctant husband towards something for which he felt ill-equipped, but I knew that God was faithful. I decided to pray that He would, in His own time and way, give Bryan the confidence he needed.

Before we could put pen to paper and become foster parents, we found out we were expecting! It was a shocking but also an exciting blessing, and we were thrilled. We decided that, after three births for which we had been overly prepared, we wanted to enjoy the surprise of this fourth (and probably last) delivery. Much to the chagrin of our family and friends, we decided not to find out the gender of baby Parris number six. We had dusty bins of tiny pink dresses and blue footie pajamas in storage. We were set. Our pregnancy, for the most part, went as expected. I had a few minor complications in the last trimester, but nothing too unexpected, and our family anxiously awaited the arrival of our newest little one.

We finally made it nine months and headed to the hospital for our planned induction. We were so ready to meet our newest little one and couldn't wait to find out the gender. At 9:57 pm that night, we welcomed sweet Neely Jane into our family. Our precious baby girl! Immediately, there was a hush in the room and an unspoken busyness. The nurses took her to the warming bed to clean her up a bit, then swaddled her and brought her to my bedside. As soon as I saw her, my heart knew. Neely was born with Down syndrome.

The next day was a whirlwind. Our hospital was not equipped to care for Neely. The pediatrician on call suspected she had a heart defect and knew that we needed to get her to our nearby children's hospital right away. He came to my room to tell me the news. He sat on the bed beside me and spoke softly and took great care with his words. He told me there were some characteristics present in our newborn baby that caused him concern. Before he could say the words, I spoke into the silence; "She has Down syndrome."

The pediatrician apologized for what he assumed had been a very restless night for me, full of worry. I assured him that I slept well and that the only concern I had was for Neely's heart. I knew as soon as I laid eyes on her that she was the answer to my prayer. Neely was God's answer to Bryan's questioning heart, wrapped up in a tiny eight-pound bundle. Who knew that confidence could come in such a sweet little package?

Neely went on to have open-heart surgery at four months, and our lives settled into a comfortable rhythm. Weekly therapies for speech, occupational, and physical needs became the norm. Our days were busy but good, but in spite of the comfortableness of those days, there was still something missing. I began to question whether God had truly called us to adoption or if He was just preparing our hearts for Neely's surprise arrival.

Over the years, I had spent countless hours on an advocacy website called Reece's Rainbow. On its pages, I found hundreds of sweet faces staring back at me. Almost all of them had Down syndrome. Whenever I started to look, I just couldn't look away. I often sent Bryan photographs of little ones I fell in love with. He always nodded and smiled at any mention of my searching. But he never stepped forward to say that it was our time to be one of those needed families. One day that all changed.

In April of 2013, I saw her face on the advocacy website. "Laura" was her name. She was a tiny sweetheart sporting a red sweatshirt that read, "That's it, I'm calling Grandma." Her face was solemn but sweet. She had the poutiest little lips, and cheeks just waiting to be kissed. I couldn't get her face out of my mind.

The next Sunday we arrived at church, only to be greeted by an empty classroom. Our small-group friends were away on vacation or out sick, and Bryan and I found ourselves alone. We sat on that overstuffed brown couch and talked about Laura.

We talked about what her future looked like, and Bryan asked lots of questions. It was heartbreaking to put into words how bleak her future really was. Here she was, only a year old, and she was already destined for a life of no expectation. No one was cheering her on to reach her goals; no one believed that she could be more than her diagnosis of Down syndrome. My heart ached for her.

As the bell rang, signaling the end of our class time, we made our way downstairs to the worship center. After the usual praise and worship time, our pastor opened his Bible and began his sermon. After only a few minutes, I no longer heard the words coming from the pulpit. I only saw the scribbled note in my husband's familiar handwriting that he slid onto my open Bible.

He asked how we could go get Laura.

Arriving at home, I stepped down out of our blue Suburban behind our little house on the hill and raced to my computer. With hands shaking, I immediately typed in the web address for the advocacy site where we saw Laura's picture. I told them that we wanted to make her our daughter and welcome her into our family. She would no longer be an orphan, but a daughter, loved and cherished. Wanted.

The next day, the adoption agency sent us her file, and we poured over every detail of her little life. That day, we submitted a letter to her home country expressing our desire to raise Laura as one of our own. Pre-approval came in a matter of weeks, and we put our nose to the grindstone to bring our daughter home. We learned her name was "MinLan," and couldn't imagine a more beautiful name for our treasured little girl.

The year passed quickly and yet, at the same time, seemed excruciatingly slow. We couldn't get our paperwork done fast enough and were devastated each time the process stalled. We filled out countless forms, submitted fingerprints, stressed, and worried. We cried tears of frustration at the smallest delay and tears of elation at each new picture or video that arrived in our inbox.

In March of 2014, Ellie and I boarded a plane to go and bring our girl home. The flight was long, but each moment in the air got us one step closer to our sweet MinLan. It had all been worth it. Every form, every phone call, every fundraiser; all of it. Our time had come to bring our baby home.

I'll never forget the moment I saw her. She absolutely took my breath away. Even though I had been looking at pictures of her for the past year, she looked so much older but, at the same time, so much smaller than I expected.

She came to me easily and gave me a smile that melted my heart. Now I know that her smile was full of pain, anxiousness, and stress, but at that moment, it was the most beautiful smile I had ever seen. At that point, there were no tears. She let me hold her close, and we completed a bit of paperwork and were off to our hotel.

When we reached our room, MinLan let us hold her but just stared at us, wide-eyed. The tears came quickly and were the most gut-wrenching sobs I have ever heard. My oldest daughter, Ellie, who had accompanied me on the trip, joined me in sobbing with MinLan. Knowing her tears came from fear and loss were heartbreaking.

MinLan quickly bonded with me, but attachment with Bryan took a bit longer. She loved her siblings and enjoyed playing with them, and her sweet giggles could light up the entire room.

We made a concentrated effort to cocoon with MinLan and establish boundaries. We were careful to discourage others from holding or feeding her, even close family and friends. I often wore her in a baby carrier and enjoyed the process of winning my daughter's heart. The shy, quiet little girl we met in China has blossomed into a silly, sassy little girl. Full of her own opinions and ideas, MinLan likes to run the show but loves her family fiercely.

On our trip to China, one of my goals was to meet some of the children remaining behind who had Down syndrome. I wanted to meet them, ask their nannies about them, and be able to return home and advocate for them. I went to the orphanage with a prepared list of names and birth dates to make my request. Our guide informed us that the nannies would bring them down after we ate our lunch with the staff. Our guide went on to ask if I minded the addition of one little boy to the list. He shared that "Timothy" was one of his favorites at the orphanage and asked if we'd like to meet him and help to find him a family. Of course, we agreed.

The children were brought into the large room, all very quiet and solemn, then lastly came a bouncing little six-year-old boy. He was full of energy, and passing out hugs with wild abandon. With my inexperience with attachment and bonding, I didn't pick up on all the signs at the time. He just seemed like a friendly, busy little boy. Soon I would be looking back and asking myself question after question about our time together that day.

We came home and began to advocate for all of the children we met on our trip, especially Timothy. Our family hosted a fundraiser around the holidays to raise funds for any family who might be willing to step forward and adopt him. He was on our minds, and we knew we had to help him find a forever home. Our children loved helping raise funds for him and even tried their best to convince Mom and Dad that we needed to adopt him. We didn't entertain their ideas in the beginning. We had just returned from the adoption of MinLan and had no plans to adopt again so quickly. But our children were determined not to give up. Our daughter Ruby Kate, who was then five, even provided us with handwritten "adoption papers" and declared that we could go get her brother.

One conversation led to the next, and we knew God was calling us to bring little Timothy home as our son. In January of 2016, Timothy became John Preston Songlang Parris.

Our second trip to China to bring John Preston home was a far stretch from the first. On this trip, I took along our oldest daughter, Ellie, and our son, Ethan, who was the same age as John Preston. Although I was nervous, I felt I was prepared, as this was our second adoption. That cool morning in January will be forever etched in my memory, but I do believe that my mind has blocked out some of the hardest parts of that time.

Shortly after we arrived at the government office to meet John Preston, we saw a peek of him in the little children's playroom. He was excited to be there, and very active. They finally introduced him to us, and he was a flurry of activity. He was excited to touch and grab for anything he could reach. He gave us all cursory hugs and continued trying to gain control of his situation.

John Preston continued to run at full throttle for the remainder of our time in China. He required two hands holding his at all times for his safety and our sanity. He enjoyed running wild if given a moment of freedom, and especially loved pushing every single button in the elevator each time we entered. I spent my days in China worried about what we had done, worried that I had taken on more than I could handle. I reached out to friends at home, adoptive mommas, and mommas I knew I could trust.

There were many times I left my children watching a cartoon in the hotel room, in a language they didn't understand, so that I could go into the bathroom and cry out to God. I knew that this journey had been a calling from the start. God had been with us every step of the way on this adoption journey. I knew that He would not call us to something for which He would not equip us. In those darkest moments, a peace began to come.

I knew that I just needed to get our family home. I knew our family would forever be different but that together we could begin the hard work of winning John Preston's heart and mending all the years of heartache that the lack of a family had brought him. Slowly, we began to see a change. Many days there was forward motion, only to see him take leaps in reverse the very next day. As a mother who felt like she had most of her life under control, this caused me to feel that I had lost my way. All the things I thought I knew were not enough to reach John Preston. I had to learn new methods, new accommodations, and new grace for each day.

John Preston has changed. But the most change came in my life. My hard and fast opinions on adoption and trauma have softened. I would never claim to understand it all or be an expert. I still struggle many days, but God has been faithful to stretch my heart and open my eyes. I have learned that the way I parented our biological children was not a perfect formula for parenting John Preston. Our biological children never knew a day where they were not loved, wanted, and treasured. They laid their heads on soft pillows at night, never doubting that their momma and daddy were right down the hall and that they were safe and protected.

Our lives are better because of adoption. Our lives are better because of one little extra chromosome. Science knows many things that I do not regarding that special twenty-first chromosome. None of that matters to me on a daily basis. It's not all perfect, but boy is it wonderful. Our three children with Down syndrome bring a light to our family that is hard to put into words. They bring life and love and more hugs than I ever thought possible. They teach us every day that hard work pays off and if you have trouble reaching your goal, you just keep trying. They have taught us about forgiveness. When someone wrongs you, love them anyway. Forgive them quickly and don't harbor anger in your heart. It's not worth the toll it takes on your own well-being.

One of the best parts of our adoption story is the effect on our children, family, and friends. Our little ones sporting an extra chromosome are world changers. Our children have learned that different is a good thing. Differences make us better people and—if we embrace them—cause us to open our hearts. I have seen our community come together to make a difference in the life of just one. I have seen people who had no connection to the Down syndrome community or adoption come together to fundraise, pray, and offer support. I've seen their hearts change before my very eyes.

Adoption and Down syndrome may seem scary to some. In the case of our family, it means a few more visits each year to specialists. It means annual blood work and testing to watch for potential issues. It means occupational, speech, and physical therapy, all to varying degrees, depending on the child. Some children need more and some very little. Some of our children will go on to college, and some will marry. Some may live at home with their parents through their adult years. The main thing to remember is that no one knows what the future holds, not with our biological children, and not with our children who came to us through adoption. No one is promised tomorrow.

What I do know for certain is that children with Down syndrome deserve the blessing of a family. Not a perfect family, not a wealthy family... just a willing family.

CHAPTER
FOURTEEN

national Down Syndrome adoption network

I first had the privilege of working with Robin Steele in 1993. I had just been hired as a secretary for the Down Syndrome Association of Greater Cincinnati (DSAGC), and Robin was one of the founding members. Her other role was founder of the National Down Syndrome Adoption Network, which is a program of the DSAGC. Robin and her husband, David, founded the NDSAN in 1982.

I provided administrative support to Robin because, back in those days, information was sent through the mail. My job was to send out information to either birth families or prospective adoptive families. Back then the highlight of my days in the office was when Robin would let me know how blessed she was to be able to comfort birth families and provide support and resources to adoptive families.

In 2010, the Executive Director asked me to take on a different role… helping the NDSAN go from a phone/mail resource to an online resource. I jumped at the chance! God provisioned me with the gift of helping others administratively, and I loved having the opportunity to help Robin put her program onto the Internet.

I got right to work on organizing the adoptive families by creating the NDSAN Registry. Robin had kept everyone's record in separate paper files. Formerly, when an agency would call and ask for specific parameters on adoptive families, Robin would have to open each file to look for those parameters. With the NDSAN Registry, we put every adoptive family into a database, and we were able to run a report for agencies within five minutes!

After creating the registry, we wanted to get the word out about the NDSAN to medical professionals who give a prenatal diagnosis of Down syndrome to expectant families. We created a booklet that talked about what Down syndrome is, and what parenting a child with Down syndrome may look like. Included were stories from birth and expectant parents, information on what making an adoption plan may look like, and resources for families.

Our purpose was this: when medical professionals give a diagnosis of Down syndrome—if they are going to offer termination as an option—we wanted families to have the option of adoption as well. The booklets were created and sent to genetic counselors, obstetricians, and Down syndrome parent groups, for use in their medical outreach programs.

We then created an online presence: www.ndsan.org. Our website is a fantastic resource for expectant parents, or for parents whose child receives a diagnosis of Down syndrome at birth. We also provide a wealth of information and resources to adoptive families who are interested in adopting a child with Down syndrome. The page that we are especially proud of is the one on which we feature and advocate for children with Down syndrome in foster care who need forever families.

We continued our online presence by creating Facebook, Instagram, LinkedIn, and Twitter pages for the NDSAN. We were ready to take on the world! Well, the United States, at least, since the NDSAN is a domestic adoption program.

And wow, did the requests for information flood in! Robin was more comfortable talking with families on the phone or via email, so I was given the task of adding new families to our registry, creating reports, and overseeing our online presence. The number of expectant and birth parent calls increased because all that families had to do was type the phrase "Down syndrome adoption" into Google, and we were the first link to appear!

The years flew by. In 2011, we helped with thirty-five adoptions, and in 2012, we had sent close to 1,000 booklets to medical professionals and pregnancy centers. In 2013, we had over 2,500 requests for information, and in 2014, forty-two adoptive families were added to the NDSAN registry.

At the end of 2014, Robin retired from the NDSAN, and I was asked to become the Director of the program in 2015. I can't describe how it felt to be given the opportunity to continue the incredible, life-changing work that Robin had done for over thirty years. It was a mixture of honor, excitement, nervousness, and just feeling absolutely blessed that I was able to work with Robin for so long, and then carry on her and David's legacy.

In 2015, the NDSAN was given the President's Award by the US Department of Child & Family Services for our work of advocating for children with Down syndrome in foster care. In 2016, we were awarded the Friend of Children Award by the North American Council on Adoptable Children for our continued work of finding families for children with Down syndrome. In 2017, the NDSAN received the President's Award by the National Down Syndrome Congress "for positively changing the lives of so many families, and for the personal commitment of providing hope to those in despair, and turning dreams into reality."

Since 2010, we have provided support to over 700 expectant or birth families whose child received a diagnosis of Down syndrome; after receiving counseling, support, or information from us, close to 300 decided to parent their child. We have also helped over 300 children with Down syndrome find their adoptive family.

The mission of the National Down Syndrome Adoption Network is "to ensure that every child born with Down syndrome has the opportunity to grow up in a loving family." To us, that means either the family who contacted us after their child was diagnosed with Down syndrome, or an adoptive family. When a family decides to parent after talking with us, our response to them is, "Congratulations!" and we refer them to their local Down syndrome parent group. If an adoptive family is chosen, we have fulfilled our mission as well, and we refer the adoptive family to their local Down syndrome parent group. We celebrate when a child finds their family, no matter who that family is.

I love my job so much. I never use the word "job"—this is a ministry to me. My vocation. A calling. My lifestyle. A service. I thank God for a "servant's heart," for the gifts of teaching, exhortation, mercy, helps, and administration. And I am beyond humbled and thankful to my Father God every day that I can minister to families. And I thank Robin and David Steele for the gift that is the National Down Syndrome Adoption Network.

- Stephanie Thompson

resource guide

resource guide inDex

225 General Adoption Information

227 Domestic Adoption

229 International Adoption

231-235 Orphan Care

237-241 Financial Assistance Organizations
for Adoptive Families

243-245 Orphan Hosting

general adoption information

These are great places to begin learning about adoption, the adoption process, and the many different options available to families:

How to Adopt

Show Hope created this website as a resource for families to help with decisions, adoption agencies, expectations, and fundraising.
www.howtoadopt.org

Christian Alliance for Orphans

This website contains a wealth of information about church and global initiatives, Orphan Sunday materials, and an extensive list of trusted nonprofit organizations.
www.cafo.org

Domestic adoption

NDSAN: National Down Syndrome Adoption Network

Adoptive families with a current, approved home study can join the registry of parents hoping to adopt a child with Down syndrome. Visit the website to watch the webinar, learn more, or find local adoption agencies to complete a home study.

www.ndsan.org

513-709-1751

stephanie@ndsan.org

Special Angels Adoption

Adoptive families with a current, approved home study can join the registry of parents hoping to adopt a child with Down syndrome or other special needs. Special Angels can also complete an adoption home study for Ohio families.

www.specialangelsadoption.org

256-452-9504

sara@specialangelsadoption.org

international adoption

Reece's Rainbow

Reece's Rainbow is not an adoption agency. The mission of Reece's Rainbow is to advocate and find families for orphans with Down syndrome and other special needs by raising funds for adoption grants. Profiles of orphans waiting for families are available for prospective adoptive families to view. Reece's Rainbow provides connections to adoption agencies with specific adoption programs in countries around the world.

www.reecesrainbow.org

Rainbow Kids

Rainbow Kids is not an adoption agency. They are a central resource linking families, adoption professionals, humanitarian organizations, orphan-care and support missions, and children living out their lives in orphanages and group homes. Rainbow Kids provides a wealth of information about country programs, international adoption agencies, waiting children profiles, and stories from adoptive families.

www.rainbowkids.com

orphan care

Families unable to adopt at this time may be interested in learning about other ways to offer support and care to orphans. These organizations work directly with children in need, providing much-needed medical care, therapy, nanny sponsorship, education, equipment, supplies, and more. Please consider helping orphans in need.

Open Hearts for Orphans

Individuals and families can contribute to the "Say Yes" adoption grants for families adopting children with Down syndrome, the Orphan Care sponsorship programs, or the Medical Interventions to help support orphans with additional medical needs. The Safe Hearts Program is an international foster care program for children that may not be orphaned, but are at risk. Sponsorship is available for foster families providing safety and care for children in need. Contributing sponsors will receive periodic updates.
www.openheartsfororphans.com

Lost Sparrows

Lost Sparrows is dedicated to improving the lives of orphans and those with special needs through education, proper medical care, and adoption.
www.lostsparrows.org

Continued ▸

orpHan care
continued

First Hugs

First Hugs helps improve the quality of life for orphans in China with special needs by providing nannies to assist with feeding, therapy, and attachment-based activities. Sponsorship of specific orphans is available.

www.firsthugs.org

Love Without Boundaries

Love Without Boundaries has a wide-reaching impact with their programs as well as transparency of where the funds are used. They provide medical care, education, foster homes, nutrition programs, healing homes, camps, specialized equipment, supplies, therapy, and special education support. LWB helps support orphans and at-risk children and families within their home country. Sponsorship is available for the many programs as well as for individual children.

www.lovewithoutboundaries.com

Lifesong for Orphans

Opportunities for giving include sponsoring an orphan, adopting an orphanage or school, and going on short-term mission trips. One hundred percent of donations go to orphan care. Lifesong also helps mobilize churches to meet local needs through foster care as well as providing grants for adoptive families.

www.lifesong.org

Continued ▸

orPHan care
continued

Show Hope

Show Hope enables you to sponsor orphan care centers, contribute to adoption grants, go on a short-term mission trip, or fundraise in your local community to raise awareness of the orphan crisis.
www.showhope.org

Tim Tebow Foundation

The foundation's Orphan Care outreach provides essentials such as food, clothing, shelter, medical care, education, and the sharing of the Gospel to orphans in several countries. One hundred percent of your orphanage donation goes directly toward orphan care.
www.timtebowfoundation.org

Reece's Rainbow

Consider donating to a child's adoption grant or supporting an adoptive family financially on their journey by contributing to the family sponsorship fund.
www.reecesrainbow.org

New Day Charities

Opportunities for sponsorship include medical care, basic needs for orphans, infant formula, or surgeries for specific children. Sponsors receive monthly updates on the child/children they are supporting.
www.newdayfosterhome.com

Financial assistance organizations for adoptive families

Adoption Bridge

Adoption Bridge, a ministry of Every Child Has a Name, brings waiting children and loving families together by bridging the gap between the emotional needs and financial challenges of adoption.

www.adoptionbridge.org

Tim Tebow Foundation

The Foundation's Adoption Aid program is focused on providing financial assistance to families adopting children with special needs.

www.timtebowfoundation.org

RODS: Racing For Orphans With Down Syndrome

A unique organization focused on raising awareness and contributing to grants for orphans with Down syndrome.

www.rods.org

Angels in Disguise

Families adopting a child with Down syndrome internationally can apply for a grant.

www.angelsindisguise.net

Ephesians 3:20 Foundation

Families can apply for financial assistance for their domestic or international adoption.

www.eph320foundation.org

Continued ▸

Financial assistance organizations for adoptive families
continued

Both Hands

The mission of Both Hands is to fulfill James 1:27 by serving orphans, widows, and Christian adoptive families. Both Hands helps adoptive families fund their adoption by coordinating service projects fixing up a widow's home.

www.bothhands.org

Brittany's Hope

The mission of Brittany's Hope is to empower families and communities to make lasting changes in the lives of orphans and at-risk children through international special needs adoption grants.

www.brittanyshope.org

Adopt Together

The world's largest crowd-funding platform for adoption.

www.adopttogether.org

Gift of Adoption Fund

Adoptive families with an approved home study can apply for an adoption assistance grant for both domestic and international adoptions.

www.giftofadoption.org

Continued ▸

Financial assistance organizations for adoptive families
continued

Room For One More Child

This organization offers adoption aid as well as providing a list of other organizations with grant opportunities.

www.roomforonemorechild.org

The Rollstone Foundation

Supports the adoption of children with special needs worldwide by providing grants to qualified prospective parents.

www.rollstone.us

Katelyn's Fund Orphan Ministry

Adoption agents are available for both domestic and international adoptions.

www.katelynsfund.org

OrPHan HOSTing

"Many people go on mission trips to other parts of the world, but we ask you to consider staying home this summer to bring the mission to your family. This experience will change the life of an orphan forever, as well as the lives of you and your children!"

-Madison Adoption Associates

Hosting orphans in your home and including them in your family activities for four to eight weeks gives orphans the experience of family life. Children have the opportunity to learn English, receive eye and dental care, and to experience how functional families and relationships work.

Consider opening your home to share love, encouragement, and hope with children in need.

Continued ▸

ORPHAN HOSTING
continued

The following are just a few organizations with orphan hosting programs.

Project 143
www.p143.org

Guglielmo's Hope
www.guglielmoshope.com

Madison Adoption Associates
www.madisonadoption.org

Every Child Has a Name
www.everychildhasaname.org

Kid Save
www.kidsave.org

A Love Beyond Borders
www.bbinternationaladoption.com

Children's House International
www.childrenshouseinternational.com

Across the World Adoptions
www.atwakids.org

acknowledgements

As the publisher, I realize that a project such as this is never a one-person effort, and I wish to thank the many people who made this book possible:

My wife, Lisa, for having the vision. Cady Driver, for all the many hours spent compiling these stories. The families, for being so willing to share their stories. Jackie Beachy Photography, for the beautiful photos for the cover. The momma's, for giving a morning (more than that, actually) for a photo shoot and allowing their sweet children be on the front cover.

- Marlin Miller
Publisher

Visit us online at:

www.extraordinaryadoption.com